HENRY WELLCOME:
The Man, his Collection and his Legacy

D1824491

HENRY WELLCOME:
The Man,
his Collection and
his Legacy

Helen Turner

THE WELLCOME TRUST
and
HEINEMANN

Published for the Wellcome Trust by
Heinemann Educational Books Ltd
22 Bedford Square, London WC1B 3HH
LONDON EDINBURGH MELBOURNE AUCKLAND
HONG KONG SINGAPORE KUALA LUMPUR NEW DELHI
IBADAN NAIROBI JOHANNESBURG
EXETER (NH) KINGSTON PORT OF SPAIN

© Helen Turner 1980
First published 1980

British Library Cataloguing in Publication Data

Turner, Helen
  Henry Wellcome.
  1. Wellcome, *Sir* Henry   2. Businessmen – Biography
  3. Collectors and collecting – Biography
  4. Philanthropists – Biography
  5. Drug trade – Great Britain – History
  338.7′61′61510924   HD9667.5

ISBN 0–435–32860–3

Printed in Great Britain by
Biddles Ltd, Guildford, Surrey

Contents

Acknowledgements

This book was commissioned by the Wellcome Trust, and the author is grateful to the Chairman of the Trustees, The Rt Hon Lord Franks, OM, and the Director of the Trust, Dr P. O. Williams, for their encouragement and guidance. Dr Brian Bracegirdle, Keeper of the Wellcome Museum of the History of Medicine at the Science Museum, his deputy, Dr Robert Anderson, and members of the staff provided advice and practical help. Special thanks are due to Mr Gilbert Macdonald of the Wellcome Foundation Limited for helpful discussions. Mr Eric Freeman, Acting Director of the Wellcome Institute for the History of Medicine, and Mr H. J. M. Symons, Assistant Librarian, supplied much of the historical material, and Dr. R. Burgess and Mr R. de Peyer of the Institute staff were also helpful. Dr A. J. Duggan of the Wellcome Museum of Medical Science kindly gave information on the history of his museum. Thanks are also due to two retired Directors of the Wellcome Foundation Ltd, Mr L. G. Matthews and Mr A. N. Falder, for their help.

Part One

Henry Wellcome, the Man

Introduction

IN September 1880 two young Americans went into partnership to found a pharmaceutical firm in London – Burroughs Wellcome & Co. Silas Burroughs died fifteen years later and full control of the expanding business passed into the hands of Henry Wellcome, to be exercised by him until his death in 1936.

Pharmacy was then relatively undeveloped, though the tide of medical research was rising through the work of such men as Lister and Pasteur. Public health had improved, yet such killer diseases as tuberculosis, typhoid and diphtheria were still unsubdued. Paul Ehrlich, the great pioneer of immunology and chemotherapy, was only 26 years of age. Pharmacists throughout Europe still used the traditional pestle and mortar and pill slab to prepare medicines. In America, however, the technique of making the new compressed pills was being perfected and it was these that Burroughs Wellcome & Co. aimed to promote on the British market.

Henry Wellcome was a forceful and astute business-man who, like many of his late Victorian contemporaries, made a great fortune from nothing. In its centenary year the Wellcome Foundation Ltd., the group of pharma-ceutical companies which grew from Burroughs Wellcome & Co., honours its founder. Wellcome has, however, other and more unusual claims to be remem-bered. Throughout his life he promoted medical research. In part, of course, he did this for sound, if unusually far-sighted, business reasons, but his idealism was also a strong motive. As a young man, he was offered the chance of going into medical practice with his uncle. Intensely ambitious and already aware of his business ability, Wellcome turned down this proposal, preferring to use wealth, rather than personal skill, in the preservation of human life and health. He made all of us his heirs through the Wellcome Trust, which is the largest non-governmental, grant-awarding body for the support of medical research in Britain, and the sole shareholder in the Foundation.

Less well known than Wellcome the businessman and patron of medical research is Wellcome the collector. His aim was to found a Museum of Man and he devoted the last twenty-five years of his life to amassing material for this ambitious purpose. It has been roughly estimated that his total collection of medical, anthropological and archaeological items must, at the time of his death, have numbered well over 1½ million. His collecting method was that of the businessman rather than the connoisseur. He bought on a huge scale, using a network of agents and contacts all over the world and acquiring whole collections wherever possible. He arranged the first public exhibition of select objects from his collection on a temporary basis in 1913 and it attracted such keen interest that he allowed it to become a permanent display. But the First World War, and his own increasing age and ill-health, prevented him from establishing the great museum he so clearly envisaged. The bulk of his collection never left its original packing cases.

On Wellcome's death, the collection became the responsibility of the Wellcome Trustees, and it has been their decision to give it on permanent loan to the Science Museum, London. Two galleries will contain on display a small but representative part of the collection. Its total quantity has been reduced since the Second World War to less than half a million items directly concerned with the history of medicine. The rest has been dispersed to other more appropriate museums and collections. That part which must still remain in store at the Science

Museum is being fully catalogued and will be available for research in due course.

So, more than forty years after his death, it is now possible for the general public to benefit more fully from a new aspect of this remarkable man's legacy. Wellcome believed deeply in the value of the study of history. He once said: 'I have found that the study of the roots and foundations of things greatly assists research, and facilitates discovery and invention.' His genius lay in the combination of two very different qualities: practical shrewdness, and idealism based on simple religious faith. At the age of 21, he wrote to his parents: 'I have always had a desire for wealth, and still have . . . but I want to live a life devoted to the true God and to mankind.' As well as the very practical results of his patronage of medical science, Wellcome bequeathed to his adopted country a unique three-dimensional record of the means Man has used through the ages to preserve and restore health.

The American Years

Henry Wellcome, who became famous in London society for his lavish and elegant entertaining, was born on a pioneer farm in the American Midwest in 1853. The seeds of some of his most dominant qualities and interests were sown during his early years. His parents, Solomon and Mary, and his paternal grandparents were deeply religious; his father and two uncles became ministers of the Adventist sect. When Henry was eight, the family, including his grandparents, decided to move from their farm in the small settlement of Almond, Wisconsin, to Garden City, Minnesota, where Jacob Wellcome, another uncle, was in medical practice. Solomon's health was failing; he needed to find lighter work and was also anxious to practise his ministry.

The journey took several weeks by covered wagon, and the Wellcomes travelled in company with a large group of other settlers, for protection from the Indians.

The Midwest in the 1860s was still frontier country. Shortly after the family had settled in Garden City, there was an uprising by the neighbouring Indian tribes. The towns became temporary fortresses manned by local volunteers as well as troops. Young Henry helped the other boys to cast bullets and also made himself

The family group, showing Henry Wellcome, his parents, seated, and his brother George, behind father, 1869.

useful to his uncle Jacob in the care of the wounded. The massacre of over 2000 settlers ended with an Indian defeat and the hanging of the tribal chiefs. These events stirred in Henry a deep sympathy for the dispossessed Indians which persisted throughout his life. His attitude to what he described as 'the subject native races' may seem patronizing to us, but showed genuine humanity and understanding. As always with Wellcome, its outcome was splendidly practical. For many years he supported Father Duncan's mission to the American Indians and his African archaeological expeditions also provided the opportunity for much social welfare work.

The move to Garden City was a fortunate one for Henry. It gave him proper schooling, the company of his uncle and cousins and his first experience of business. Jacob Wellcome owned a drug store attached to his consulting rooms and Solomon became the manager with active help from Henry. When he was only 16 the first Wellcome product appeared on the market and set the pattern for the future by being cleverly advertised. The advertisement ran:

Wellcome's Magic Ink

THE GREATEST WONDER OF THE AGE!

This is something entirely New and Novel!

DIRECTIONS

Write with a quill or golden pen on white paper.
No trace is visible until held to the fire, when
it becomes very black.

Prepared only by
H. S. WELLCOME,
Garden City, Minn.

Though the drug store was, in the American style, a general shop rather than a chemist's as we know it, Henry Wellcome did learn the rudiments of pharmacy from an English pharmacist who was working in the town. At the same time his interest in medicine was stimulated both by his uncle, whom he deeply admired, and by Jacob's close friend Dr William Mayo, whose sons founded the famous Mayo Clinic in Rochester, Minnesota. It was in Rochester that Henry took his first job, at the age of 17, with the firm of Poole & Geisenger, pharmaceutical chemists. His aim was to work his way through college and with this in view he found work first in Chicago and then in Philadelphia, where in 1874 he graduated from the Philadelphia College of Pharmacy. Just how much determination these years of study demanded is shown by a letter he wrote home from Philadelphia: 'I have not bought a rag of clothes since I came to the city, and have not a whole pair of pants or boots to my name. Have had to wear rubbers over my boots to keep them together.' The choice which now faced Wellcome – he had already rejected medicine in the form of his uncle's offer of a partnership – was whether to make money fast in the expanding west or go east to learn more of business methods. He chose the latter and joined the New York firm of Caswell Hazard & Co., where he set about making himself known in his profession through his active membership of the American Pharmaceutical Association. He read several papers to the Association, and was elected a member of its Standing Business Committee. In 1876 came the opportunity he had been waiting for, a letter from the leading American pharmaceutical firm of McKesson & Robbins which read: 'We have decided to give you a trial if you can start immediately . . . The salary we offer is 16 dollars per week, and expenses paid while you are on the road for us.' Wellcome accepted the offer to become a travelling salesman for the new gelatine-coated pills which the firm was promoting to the medical profession and to druggists. His journeys were considerably more adventurous than those of most commercial travellers, taking him into the remote parts of South America. His energy, physical courage and organizing ability made travel in remote areas particularly congenial, and it remained so throughout his life. While travelling in Peru and Ecuador he made a special study of the cinchona forests through which he passed because of their growing importance in the production of quinine. His first-hand observations on the preparation of cinchona bark were published in the Proceedings of the American Pharmaceutical Association and in the Pharmaceutical Journal of Great Britain, where they attracted wide interest.

By 1879 Wellcome had a high reputation as a pharmaceutical salesman and was well known in the profession. Meanwhile his former college friend, Silas Burroughs, was doing similar work for the Philadelphia firm of John Wyeth & Brother and had just established himself in London as Wyeths' agent. Not long after his arrival in England, he asked Wellcome to join him in a business partnership for the promotion of compressed medicines. 'I think we would make a pretty lively team in the pharmaceutical line', he wrote.

Wellcome's interest was obvious but he was cautious as ever. He decided to visit Europe before committing himself and arranged with McKesson & Robbins that he should go to Europe on their account. He told his employers of Burroughs' proposal and they advised him to accept, while offering him a considerable increase in salary if he decided to stay with the firm. In April 1880, he received a contract from McKesson & Robbins giving him exclusive agency for their products in 'Europe, Asia, Africa, East Indies and Australia'. The contract contained a clause which provided that 'H. S. Wellcome may associate himself with partners . . . in which case this agreement will apply to such firm while Mr Wellcome is with it'. Clearly the partnership idea appealed strongly to Wellcome but he was sufficiently wise to make provision for an independent future should the partnership prove unsatisfactory. Wellcome arrived in London in May and reached a basic understanding with Burroughs on the terms of the partnership. However Wellcome insisted that before signature Burroughs must obtain the consent of Wyeths'. So during the summer Burroughs returned to Philadelphia, while Wellcome made a tour of Europe. The deed of partnership between the two men was executed on 27 September 1880 and the firm of Burroughs Wellcome & Company was established as from the first of that month.

The Making of the Business

The firm of Burroughs Wellcome & Co. was started in the right place at the right time by two men fully equipped to seize their opportunity. There were no big manufacturing chemists in Britain, no chains of chemists' shops, and large scale pharmaceutical production was limited to a few well-known lines. The new compressed tablets from America, with their accurately measured and easily administered doses, only needed to be made known and available for their sale to be assured.

The making known presented few problems to Wellcome whose flair for publicity was one of his most valuable business assets. He realized that the essentials of successful advertising are to create an acceptable image and to make sure that no opportunity is lost for presenting it to the public. And he also knew that successful advertising means spending a lot of money. From the very first year of trading, Burroughs Wellcome & Co. made its mark by extensive advertising in trade papers and professional journals and by exhibition stands which attracted the maximum attention wherever the firm hoped to market its products. Indirect advertising included the firm's involvement with important medical or scientific conferences and international hospitality

Henry Wellcome the publicist, wearing a cowboy hat, beside the Burroughs Wellcome stand at the Chicago Trade Fair, 1893.

with which the name of Burroughs Wellcome was discreetly associated. Wellcome became famous for his splendidly arranged banquets, one of the most memorable of which was the Thanksgiving Day banquet of the American Society in London in 1896. Wellcome was the chairman of the Society and he arranged the whole event, including the presentation to each guest of a handsome leather-bound volume containing a souvenir menu and an illustrated history of the discovery of America. The quality and style which Wellcome made the hallmark of all his publicity naturally became associated with the firm's products.

Once Burroughs Wellcome & Co. started to manufacture their own goods, a suitable brand name became of paramount importance. Wellcome coined, in 1884, what is arguably the most famous trade name in all business history, 'Tabloid'. In 1908, he kept pace with the growth of visual advertising by devising the Burroughs Wellcome unicorn emblem. But the most characteristic of his advertising ploys was his promotion of the 'Tabloid' medicine chest. Compressed medicines were, of course, ideal for travellers, and the Edwardians were the most intrepid of explorers, missionaries and mountaineers. Wellcome made sure that there was no national or international personality, from kings, presidents and prime ministers to cricket captains, who was not equipped with a 'Tabloid' chest. H. M. Stanley, the rescuer of Dr Livingstone, was the recipient of the very first chest in 1887. King Edward VII, King George V, Gladstone and President Theodore Roosevelt, all had one. Chests went to the North and South Poles, to Everest, and on the flights of the pioneer aviators. Each time one was presented, Wellcome made sure that everyone knew about it.

So it is not surprising that, within a short time, Wellcome was writing: 'We have now opened up businesses nearly all over the world'. By 1883 larger premises were needed and the firm acquired Snow Hill Buildings, which was to be the headquarters of

Drawing of the interior of Snow Hill building, as designed by Henry Wellcome, 1888.

Burroughs Wellcome & Co. until 1941, when it was bombed. It was one of the earliest business houses in London to introduce the new electric light.

The partners quickly realized that to market American imports would be to sacrifice most of their potential in the world market. Stamp duty made importing uneconomic, so clearly Burroughs Wellcome must begin its own manufacturing enterprise. A factory was acquired at Wandsworth and it was to deal with the problem of imitations of the compressed products they made that Wellcome registered the name 'Tabloid'. In 1886 Wellcome's health broke down and he took an enforced holiday in the forests of Maine, USA, canoeing, camping and hunting. This return to the surroundings of his childhood renewed his interest in the Indians and he wrote *The Story of Metlakahtla,* based on the mission of his friend, Father William Duncan, to the Indian tribe of that name. The book was a success, selling three editions in a few weeks, and Wellcome donated all the profits to Father Duncan's work.

Returning to business with fresh vigour, Wellcome found that the Wandsworth factory was proving too small. He and Burroughs disagreed on the next step, for Wellcome wanted to keep production in Britain, while Burroughs wanted to transfer the manufacturing side of the business to America. Wellcome had his way, and acquired a former paper mill at Dartford, where the Thames barges could be used for transport. Wellcome's practical bent came into its own in the complete equipping of the new factory with the latest labour-saving machinery.

So far only passing mention has been made of Silas Burroughs, who gave Wellcome the vital opportunity to become his own master. The partnership lasted for only fifteen years and was actually terminated by Burroughs' early death from pleurisy in 1895. It would probably have ended anyway, for as early as 1889 Burroughs' solicitors had served a writ on Wellcome for the dissolution of the partnership on the curious grounds of 'neglect of the firm's interests'. Not surprisingly judgment was given in Wellcome's favour, the judge remarking, 'I don't see any grounds for a dissolution'.

There was, in fact, no legal, or indeed logical reason why Burroughs and Wellcome should not have formed an admirable combination. Both were gifted and energetic. Burroughs was an extrovert, charming and likeable, whose foreign tours brought much business to the firm. He was much loved by all the staff of the company while Wellcome was held in respect and awe. Burroughs lacked Wellcome's industry, determination and far-sightedness, but his contribution to the success of Burroughs Wellcome & Co. was a valuable one. The root of the differences between the two men lay, almost certainly, in jealousy. Wellcome, believing with some justice that his contribution to building up the business was the greater, wanted to make all the decisions, to be in complete control. Burroughs could not stomach this, and tried with increasing irrationality to thwart Wellcome's plans for the firm. The souring of their relationship over a number of years made it inevitable that Wellcome's reaction to Burroughs' sudden death should be relief. He wrote: 'By the rule of Fate, I have become sole proprietor of this great business into which I have put my heart and the best years of my life. I feel even with the added responsibility, in one sense, a wonderful relief from the strain of worry that has weighed me down so long.'

The period from Burroughs' death to the outbreak of the First World War was one of massive expansion for the company and Wellcome himself became the leading figure in the British pharmaceutical industry. Overseas the business grew rapidly. The Sydney house had opened in 1886 and the new century saw offices opened in Cape Town, Milan, New York, Montreal, Shanghai, Buenos Aires and Bombay. Wellcome travelled widely, always anxious to assess each country's needs at first hand. At European engineering centres he studied the newest manufacturing plant and was quick to see how it could

Henry Wellcome, circa 1895.

be adapted for use in his own factories. During the first five years of the twentieth century Wellcome was involved in a battle against fradulent substitution by other pharmaceutical firms. Because of the high quality of Burroughs Wellcome products, other manufacturers, not only in Britain but in other parts of the world, found it profitable to market their goods under descriptions which infringed Burroughs Wellcome & Co.'s registered trade mark. In September 1900 a successful case was fought against three pharmacists in Milan, and in 1902 two more actions were won in Britain. The culmination was the case of Burroughs Wellcome & Co. v. Thompson & Capper in 1903–4, which made history as the 'Tabloid' case.

The action was brought against Thompson & Capper of Liverpool for passing off goods not manufactured by Burroughs Wellcome & Co. under that firm's trade name. The defendants claimed that the trade mark 'Tabloid' was a descriptive word, and as such a bad trade mark. The prosecution relied upon two main contentions: that doctors prescribed 'Tabloid' products specifically because they relied upon the purity and accuracy of Burroughs Wellcome & Co.'s products; and that the word 'Tabloid' is not descriptive but was invented by Wellcome and generally recognized solely to denote a product of his firm. The problem was that the name had come into general use to mean anything in compressed or compact form.

Wellcome himself was in the witness box for most of two days. He was quite unshakable under cross examination, indeed his tenacity and quick wit made the firm's victory a personal triumph. The defendants went to appeal on the use of the trade mark alone but the Court of Appeal upheld the lower court's judgement, the President of the Court saying: 'I think that the word ['Tabloid'] is a fancy word and that it is a coined word; I think that it did not describe anything intelligibly in 1884 to those who heard it.' In fact the word 'Tabloid' has passed into general use but it is defined in the Shorter

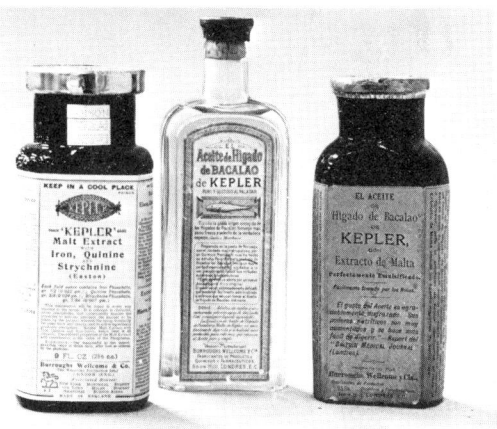

Burroughs Wellcome products, showing the trade name, Tabloid, and labels printed in Portuguese.

Oxford Dictionary as the invention and property of Burroughs Wellcome & Co.

After 1905, Wellcome began generally to devote less time to the day-to-day running of the firm. For twenty-five years it had absorbed the major part of his time and thought but now his scientific, archaeological, and collecting interests were allowed to take over. Yet he never failed, even when he was over 70, to grapple with any serious problem that arose in the Wellcome empire. As late as 1927 he was told that criticisms were being made of the high price of Wellcome products in Canada, as compared with the price of the same goods in the United States. He immediately decided to investigate the Canadian situation and concluded that manufacturing must be established at once in that country. Letters he wrote to London from Canada at the time give a valuable summary of his business philosophy:

> When we pioneered and introduced anti-diphtheritic serum in the United Kingdom, we supplied it at a price very much below cost, for a considerable time, until we had developed improved processes which reduced the cost of production and increased the volume of output to a point that enabled us to take a fair profit.
>
> In pioneering new territories I adopted the same principle by expending freely but with deliberately considered methods of effectual propaganda for a term of years – and at a loss when necessary – until we established a favourable reputation and created a volume of business that covered expenses and finally yielded substantial profits. In some new territories it took ten years or more of patient, persistent and strenuous enterprise before we secured net profits.
>
> We did not attempt to capture the whole universe at one stroke, but selected one field at a time for thorough treatment, until we had won a secure footing and substantial returns for our efforts and expenditures in the selected field. In each case we continued our propaganda in regions already covered and used funds from the income derived from the already successfully developed countries for cultivating a new and untilled field. It was thus that we gained our world wide repute and success.
>
> In all business undertakings it is a sound principle and always an essential practice for the sake of security, to keep under close observation and continuous check the question of profit and loss as well as the account of sales, expenses, taxes, etc. However, an accountant's

view that immediate profits are the all-essential points for consideration in promoting the development and best interests of the business, may not prove to be the most practical policy in building up a successful business, especially in pioneer fields.

Patron and Amateur of Science

Today it is recognized that research is a natural accessory to the manufacture of pharmaceuticals, and indeed many other products. In 1894, when Henry Wellcome opened the first of his research laboratories, such an idea was both unusual and ambitious. But Wellcome's decision to promote research was wise in business terms, as well as a vital means of furthering his humanitarian ideals. Because of his belief in the absolute value of research he gave his scientific staff liberal terms of reference. The result was that he gathered men of great ability into his employ. In the years before the First World War the Wellcome Physiological Research Laboratories were headed by Dr (later Sir) Henry Dale, who became a Nobel prize winner, a member of the Order of Merit and President of the Royal Society. Seven of his colleagues eventually became Fellows of the Royal Society. It was in these laboratories that the discovery was made of the body's capacity to provide anti-toxin more and more efficiently by the repeated injection of small quantities of toxin at suitable intervals. This discovery led to improvements in the production of anti-toxin in horses for the treatment of diphtheria, tetanus and gas-gangrene. Dr A. T. Glenny, FRS, who spent his working life in research for the Wellcome organization, was the first to advocate the use of toxoid for diphtheria immunization of children. A toxoid is a bacterial toxin modified by treatment so that it no longer kills an animal when injected but still induces the formation of anti-toxin. Glenny devised the preparation APT which became the standard preparation for diphtheria immunization in this country and other parts of the world. Glenny's successors, Dr O'Brien and Dr H. J. Parish, played major roles in the planning of the mass immunization campaign launched by the Ministry of Health in Britain in 1940 which led to a dramatic reduction in the incidence of diphtheria.

The Wellcome Physiological Research Laboratories began work in modest premises in Charlotte Street, London, with stables for eight horses nearby. In 1898 they moved to Brockwell Hall, Herne Hill, and in 1921 to Beckenham in Kent, which is still the home of the Wellcome Research Laboratories. In 1900–1, Wellcome's determination and astuteness won him a considerable victory on behalf of the Physiological Research Laboratories. This was official permission for the Laboratories to carry out experimental work on live animals, under, of course, carefully controlled conditions. Without this facility, which enabled anti-toxins to be tested, many of today's life-saving drugs would never have emerged. Until that date no private research institution had been given such authorization and the decision was a seal

Brockwell Hall, Herne Hill, used as the Wellcome Physiological Research Laboratories, 1898–1922.

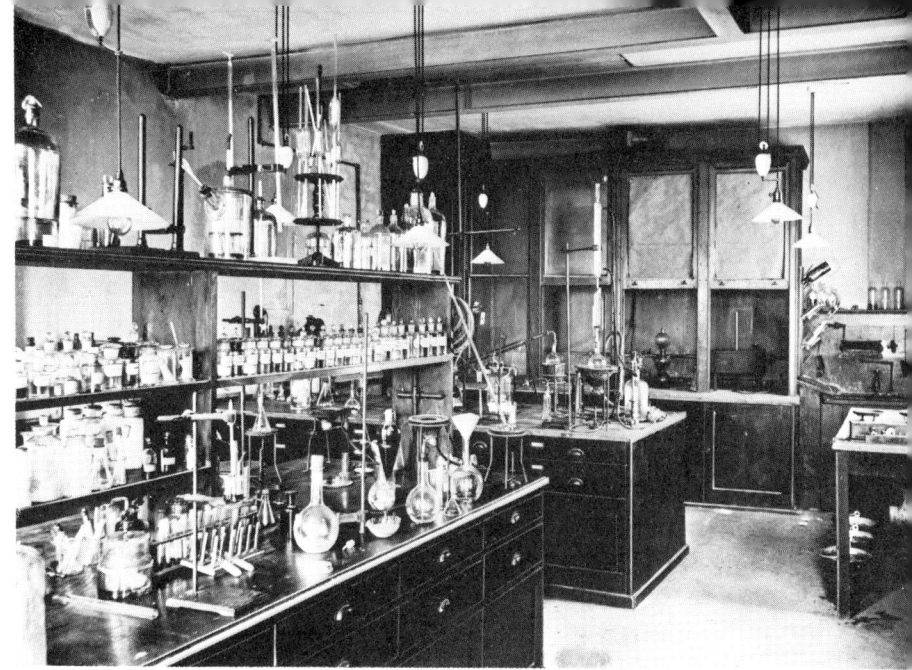

Interior of the Wellcome Chemical Research Laboratory, when at
6 King Street, Snow Hill, post-1899.

of approval on the quality of scientific work at the
Laboratories.

Many years before, when Wellcome was a student in
Philadelphia, he became friendly with a fellow student
called Frederick Power who subsequently had a distinguished career as a chemist. In 1896 Wellcome decided
to found Chemical Research Laboratories and he invited
his friend to become the director. As always with his
scientific appointments, Wellcome offered Power full
freedom to pursue any line of research he chose and to
publish the results. With the foundation of this, the
second of his laboratories, Wellcome was again at pains
to make it publicly clear that their commercial function
was secondary to their scientific purpose. *The Times* of
11 July 1900 reported:

> Though Mr Wellcome is a member of the firm of
> Burroughs Wellcome & Co., and does not disguise
> the fact that some of the work done has reference to
> the requirements of the firm, still from the nature of
> the researches already carried out, it is obvious that
> the laboratories are not ordered in any narrow

commercial spirit, and are engaged in many purely scientific enquiries that have no direct commercial significance.

In eighteen years' work with the Wellcome Chemical Research Laboratories, Frederick Power was associated with seventy-five scientific papers in chemistry and pharmacology. His plant investigations led to the discovery of the drug that had some success in the treatment of leprosy until it was replaced, more than thirty years later, by the first sulphone derivatives, which were also discovered in the Wellcome laboratories. Dr Power's reputation was such that he was asked to revise both the British and the United States' Pharmacopoeias.

Over the years many important chemical and pharmacological results have come from the Wellcome Laboratories. These included the isolation of histamine, an important terminal link in the chain of causation of allergic reactions, which later resulted in the production of the antihistamines; and the standardization of the dosage of insulin, the first producers of which in Britain were Burroughs Wellcome.

It may not be generally realized that ever since 1900 Burroughs Wellcome & Co. has been engaged in the field of veterinary medicine. The firm's medical products price list for that year includes reference to a range of sixteen veterinary, 'Tabloid'-brand, hypodermic products, including such drugs as morphine, digitalis and cocaine. It was, however, in the 1920s that the Wellcome organization became significantly involved in veterinary research. It was then that Thomas Dalling, who joined the firm to care for the laboratory horses, went on to carry out his important research on the treatment of lamb dysentery. A form of immunization against this disease was developed which reduced the very heavy death toll of new-born lambs to almost nil. Dalling was also engaged in developing vaccines against canine and feline distemper and feline enteritis. Livestock as different as poultry and race horses have also benefited from vaccines developed in the Wellcome Research Laboratories.

Henry Wellcome's personal interest in African affairs led to the setting up of another most important branch of research, that into tropical diseases. At the end of the nineteenth century the eyes of the world were focused on the Sudan, following the death of General Gordon at Khartoum. In 1898 General Kitchener avenged the murder of Britain's hero by finally defeating the Mahdi's forces at Omdurman. Two years later Wellcome travelled to the Sudan to see for himself how great was the task of rehabilitating the vast and war-torn country. He was so horrified by the disease and misery he witnessed that in 1901 he made a formal offer to Sir Reginald

Henry Wellcome on the Nile, during his visit to the Sudan, 1900–1901

Wingate, Governor-General of the Sudan, to finance the setting up of tropical research laboratories in Khartoum. The offer was gratefully accepted and Andrew Balfour was appointed the first director. Balfour, as medical officer of health as well as director of the laboratories, organized the health service of Khartoum and succeeded in transforming the dusty, insanitary mud huts into a model settlement from which he eliminated malaria. Wellcome saw to it that Balfour's reports on the progress of his work were published and made available internationally, and they became standard works in the field of tropical medicine. In 1907 Wellcome added to the resources of the laboratories a research boat which could be used on the Nile to carry medical teams into regions otherwise inaccessible.

The final development of Wellcome's research activity was the foundation in 1913 of the Wellcome Bureau of Scientific Research in London, designed as a centre for the study of tropical diseases. Dr Andrew Balfour returned home from the Sudan to become its director and at the same time he was appointed director-in-chief

The Wellcome floating laboratory on the Nile, with its tug, the Culex, *1907.*

of the other Wellcome research units. He was succeeded in 1923 by Dr C. M. Wenyon, a pathologist and proto-zoologist, who had been in charge of the floating laboratory on the Nile. In the years after the First World War, the work of the Wellcome Bureau of Scientific Research included important studies of sleeping sickness and the development of an effective vaccine against yellow fever.

Mention has already been made of the important work carried out at the Wellcome Research Laboratories on the standardization of insulin. One of the problems in preparing insulin was that it was difficult to determine the amount actually present in the prepared material. No chemical method was known for the identification or assay of insulin; and in the absence of a chemical test reliance was placed on measuring the effect on mice or rabbits. This method, however, soon produced difficul-ties, because it was found that individual mice and rabbits varied enormously in their sensitivity to insulin. The measurement of the activity of a given sample of insulin had therefore to be treated as a problem requiring statistical method. In this way, a new subject of study was created, biological assay, leading to a complete change of outlook and method. Burroughs Wellcome & Co. revolutionized the methods of standard-izing medicine. Crude medicaments were superseded by products of definite therapeutic activity controlled by chemical and physiological tests. Wellcome introduced standardization of alkaloids at the turn of the century, based on assay of the active principle rather than, as was common practice, relying on total alkaloid content. It was Wellcome's insistence on purity and accuracy which led his firm to anticipate the standards and tests now enforced by regulatory authorities such as the committees set up by the Medicines Commission in Britain and the Food and Drugs Administration in the USA.

Henry Wellcome's interest in archaeology began in his boyhood, and was closely associated with his love of collecting and his sympathy for the American Indians. In later life the same feeling of sympathy for the oppressed and the desire to do something practical to help them was awakened by his travels in the Sudan. In 1910, he was asked by Kitchener whether he could offer further help in providing for the welfare of the Sudanese, whom he had already helped by the foundation of the Tropical Research Laboratories. Wellcome's response was to start a programme of excavation at a site called Jebel Moya, midway between the Blue and the White Nile. For four years he spent most of his time in Africa and ruled over an army of native labourers which increased from 500 in the first season to 3000 in the fourth. There can be little doubt that Wellcome knew a good deal more about organizing a work-force, and improving health and living conditions, than he did about archaeological excavation. However, the finds at Jebel Moya, dating from 1000–400 BC, made a significant contribution to the history of the Middle East. In 1932 Wellcome largely financed another archaeological expedition, which investigated an ancient mound twenty-five miles south-west of Jerusalem, now generally accepted as the site of the Amorite city of Lachish. Here documents were found dating from before 587 BC which are thought to relate to the life of the Biblical prophet Jeremiah.

Mankind his Heirs

Henry Wellcome's collecting activities, which were his keenest and most continuing interest in the last years of his life, are described later in this book. Apart from this, the period from 1920 to his death in 1936 can be seen as one of consolidation and forward planning. All his life Wellcome prided himself, with reason, on his far-sightedness and his capacity to anticipate and prepare for future developments. Always a hard worker, his activity intensified rather than diminished in the years when many people plan to relax in retirement. With no

Henry Wellcome looking down on the excavations at Jebel Moya,
circa *1913.*

individual to whom he could hand over his empire, he used his last years to make suitable arrangements for mankind to benefit from his life's work.

The first step towards this was the registration, on 1 January 1924, of the Wellcome Foundation Ltd as a private company with a capital of £1 million. This firm was to co-ordinate all the branches of Burroughs Wellcome & Co in Britain and abroad, and the associated scientific and research institutions. It was necessary for all the principal overseas branches to be incorporated as separate private companies, owned by the Foundation. This business reorganization sounds simple when stated in these very general terms. In fact it was both complex and difficult, particularly the association of the research institutions with the business. Wellcome's choice of the name 'Foundation' also caused, and continues to cause, some confusion, because it carries the meaning of a charity rather than a business concern.

The varied and scattered laboratories and museums which now formed part of the Foundation urgently needed a permanent home, preferably one specially built for the purpose. The war delayed plans to build, but in 1930 a site was bought in Euston Road, London, and at the end of 1931 the foundation stone of the Wellcome Research Institution was laid. It was intended that the building should house the Bureau of Scientific Research, the Chemical Research Laboratories, and the two Wellcome Museums: the Historical Medical Museum and the Museum of Medical Science. The Physiological Research Laboratories and the Entomological Research Laboratories (founded 1920) remained in their existing rural locations at Beckenham and Esher.

Wellcome's lifelong interest in the American Indians and his friendship with Father William Duncan have already been referred to. His support of Duncan's mission did not end with the writing of his book, *The Story of Metlakahtla*. As Duncan grew older, his thriving settlement for the Indians in Alaska was threatened by speculators. Wellcome immediately went to his assistance and provided legal advice. Following Duncan's death in 1918 Wellcome acted as a trustee of his estate and finally succeeded in persuading the United States Senate to carry out a survey of conditions among the Indians. This was not simply patronage by remote control. Wellcome spent time and energy, as well as money, and his personal involvement was an enormous asset to the cause of the American Indians.

His other important philanthropic interest was in missionary work in Uganda, where he supported the maternity welfare work of the Cook family. In 1927 he gave the money to build a maternity and child welfare centre. The building, which at his request was called 'The Lady Stanley Women's Hospital', was opened in 1931.

Full recognition of Wellcome as a patron of science and a philanthropist came late in his life, but began, very appropriately, with an honorary degree in 1903 from the Philadelphia College of Pharmacy, where he had been a student. He was made an honorary Doctor of Laws by Edinburgh University in 1928 and the Society of Apothecaries of London made him a Freeman in 1931. His knighthood was conferred in 1932, an honour which his naturalization as a British subject in 1910 made possible and which many people considered to be over-due. Perhaps the honour which pleased him most was his election, also in 1932, as an honorary Fellow of the Royal College of Surgeons, a very rare distinction for anyone not holding a medical degree, and one which he knew indicated the high respect in which he was held by the medical profession. The same year he was elected a Fellow of the Royal Society for 'conspicuous services to the cause of science'.

Throughout their lives Henry Wellcome's parents and his brother George were cared for, and visited whenever possible; and the town where he was brought up was never forgotten. In 1913 Wellcome made the first moves towards creating a memorial to his parents in Garden City, Minnesota, and land was gradually purchased that included the site of the Wellcome drug store. When a new school was needed for the town, Wellcome made the necessary land available from his holding, and his will provided for the completion of his memorial plans.

Wellcome died in 1936 after a short illness. He lives on through his remarkable will, which established the Wellcome Trust. All the shares in the Foundation were vested in five Trustees nominated by the will. Profits declared as dividends were to be used for 'the advancement of research work bearing upon medicine, surgery, chemistry, physiology, bacteriology, therapeutics, materia medica, pharmacy and allied subjects'. The terms of the will also provided for the establishment or endowment of research museums or libraries and for the collection of information connected with the history of medicine. The will was the first example in Britain of a bequest by which the profits from a great trading concern are permanently dedicated to the advancement of knowledge for the benefit of mankind.

'Henry Wellcome . . . was curiously lonely'

These were the words used by Sir Henry Dale, one of Wellcome's closest associates in his later years, in an obituary tribute written for *The Times*. The quotation continues: 'It may be doubted whether anyone knew him with sufficient intimacy to do more than speculate as to his real feelings and motives.' Yet Henry Wellcome was far from a recluse, particularly in his younger days. He achieved an enviable place in London society in the 1880s and 1890s. In 1882 he wrote to Silas Burroughs:

> I wish very much you could have been with us on 17th July. We had some magnificent singing and instrumental music, recitations, etc. Among our friends present were many eminent in literature, music, drama and art, but what would have most pleased your fancy – so many really handsome girls . . .

The house I occupy is one of those on Marylebone Road, about two blocks above Baker Street (second door from the Tussauds' private residence). A handsome garden in front which I improved. This house was formerly occupied by an Indian rajah and is rather elaborately, in fact barbarously decorated inside – but as barbaric decoration is now the rage, it is in perfect accord with high art of the day. I fitted up the house to correspond in general style and quaintness. My collection of curiosities, Indian relics, etc. tally admirably with the house, and so everybody seems rather fascinated at the effect, and in fact I rather like it myself. Some call it 'aesthetic', some say 'heathenish', some 'bohemian', 'ideal', 'artistic', etc., etc.

In 1884, he was described by the magazine *Society* as 'the genial and courteous host'. He was rather a lion-hunter and he delighted in arranging ambitious functions. Yet, gregarious and sociable though he was, he does not seem, even as a young man, to have made many close friendships. The most intimate was with Henry Morton Stanley, the explorer. The two men had much in common and Stanley possessed the qualities of physical courage, enterprise and integrity which Wellcome most admired. Stanley too had spent his early years in America and had achieved fame from even humbler beginnings than Wellcome, for he was brought up in an orphan asylum. The two men shared a passion for travel in remote parts of the world and a deep interest in Africa. Wellcome was a great support to Stanley during the period when he suffered public criticism following the Second Column disaster. The two men became very close during Stanley's last illness and Wellcome wrote the foreword to Lady Stanley's life of her husband.

The younger Wellcome clearly possessed the qualities of pride and reserve which made him difficult to know well but he also had a taste for company and the capacity for friendship. What changed him into the rather forbidding figure whom no one felt they could get to know well, was the tragedy of his marriage. He was 48 when, in 1901, he married Gwendoline Syrie Barnardo, the 21-year-old daughter of Dr Thomas Barnardo, famous for his social work among the poor children of London's East End. The two met while travelling in the Sudan in the early months of 1901 and their marriage took place in London in the summer. Syrie was a strikingly beautiful woman, and both clever and ambitious. After the end of her second marriage, to the writer W. Somerset Maugham, she made a successful career as an interior decorator. Wellcome was a celebrity, rich, successful in business, sought after socially. Each must have seen in the other much to admire, but they had not allowed time to get to know each other, and the generation-wide difference in their ages was a serious barrier. At first all went well. They travelled together, set up house at Hayes in Kent, and a son was born in 1903. The family had a successful visit to America in 1905, when Mr and Mrs Wellcome were received in Washington by President Theodore Roosevelt. Less happy was their next transatlantic journey, for while they were in Central America in 1909

The first home of Henry Wellcome and his wife, The Oast House, Hayes, Kent, 1902–4.

with a party of friends a serious quarrel took place and Syrie left for New York with a friend. Wellcome and Syrie never met again. After six years of separation, during which Wellcome made his wife a most generous allowance, a divorce was granted, with Wellcome having custody of their son, Mounteney. In 1910, soon after the separation, he wrote to a friend:

> I shall try to drown my sorrow in work. Work is a great comforter, and my life work is one that contributes to the welfare of others, as well as myself, and this thought helps to brighten one's life. I hope to find happiness in guiding little Mounteney in his life and education, and in helping to shape his career.

This last satisfaction was denied him, for Mounteney was unsuited by temperament and ability to follow his father in business and to be his heir. He was brought up quietly in the country, though father and son met regularly and travelled abroad together.

So it was that in his early 60s Henry Wellcome was left without family or friends capable of sharing his deepest interests. For the rest of his life he found satisfaction in work, in pursuing his many interests, and in travelling. He was a public man, armoured against personal relationships, so that even those who knew him well never felt close to him.

Throughout his life his hobbies were physical ones. In his youth he greatly enjoyed swimming and canoeing and he was actually awarded the bronze medal of the Royal Humane Society for his rescue of a companion after a boating accident on the Thames. Later, motoring became a keen hobby and in 1907 he went on a motor tour of France, Spain and Portugal, a highly adventurous expedition in those early days. Frequent cables arrived at Snow Hill Buildings requiring urgent delivery by passenger train of tyres, new springs, valves and other motoring accessories. In later years one of his pleasures was to drive early vintage cars.

Henry Wellcome on a motoring holiday with friends in Kent, 1906.

There are still a number of people alive who remember Henry Wellcome as an older man. The remarkable thing about their personal reminiscences of Wellcome is how little they have to tell. He was always aloof; courteous, prepared to listen to another point of view, but entirely unyielding once he had made his own decision. A favourite saying of Wellcome's was: 'Never tell anyone what you propose to do until you have done it'. He was unforgiving to anyone who had seriously crossed or angered him.

Though he had many other activities besides his business, he turned them all into work, for he seldom, if ever, relaxed. His attention to detail was fantastic and operated on everything he dealt with, important and unimportant. He liked to have decisions referred to him and each subject was then placed under the searchlight of his detailed scrutiny, whether it were the design of the hind leg of the company's unicorn emblem or the colour of the paint for the walls of the Wellcome Museum of Medical Science, to which twenty-six coats were applied before he was satisfied. He maintained his house in Gloucester Gate until his death but seldom lived there for any length of time. However the care-taker always received meticulous instructions on the food to be provided for his three cats. One can imagine Wellcome liking cats and respecting their aloof independence.

However much Wellcome held other people at arm's length, few, if any, failed to respond to his qualities. The comment of one of his former staff: 'He was a great man and I was proud to work for him', would have been echoed by nearly everyone who knew him. His own phrase 'in pursuit of excellence' epitomized the quality in him which most of all commanded admiration. Greatness lies not so much in achievement as in an innate quality of personality, and this it is clear Wellcome possessed.

Part Two

The Collection

A Born Collector

HENRY Wellcome began to collect early in his life, and before 1900 he had already conceived the idea of a museum of the history of medicine. His collecting was no mere pointless acquisition nor solely a means of deploying his great wealth, which he had no immediate family to share and inherit. His objective was the creation of a museum, and he had thought deeply about the nature and purpose of what he planned to create. Though his ideas may seem to us grandiose, and in fact proved impossible of achievement on the scale he envisaged, this by no means invalidates the concept.

In 1928 Wellcome gave evidence before the Royal Commission on National Museums and Galleries. The questions he was asked drew from him clear and detailed comments on the role and organization of museums and on his plans for his own collection. He was well aware of the two, sometimes contradictory functions of museums: to provide entertainment with education for the casual visitor and to offer to the serious student material for historical research. He sought to satisfy both these needs, which is not as simple as might be thought. The general public is best served by a comparatively small number of carefully chosen objects, attractively displayed, and with ample explanatory labelling. The scholar requires access to a far wider range of artefacts. Monetary value, artistic quality and completeness are not of primary importance, and duplication is a positive advantage, since items should be handled as well as looked at. Wellcome, in fact, had fully grasped the essential qualities of a research museum. It should offer archive material of all kinds, three-dimensional objects, paintings, printed books and manuscripts, and ephemera, such as advertisements and trade labels. So his library, though now physically separate from the museum, is in conception an integral part of it. Wellcome saw his museum as nothing less than a museum of the history of Man. As he told the Royal Commission:

> Actually my interest in anthropology came before the medical, but still they have both continued on parallel lines or have been merged. My collections of anthropological material, considered as such, are vastly greater than the strictly medical, while most of the anthropological material possesses strong medical significance, for in all the ages the preservation of health and life has been uppermost in the minds of living beings, hence the omnipresent medicine man and the religio-medico or priest-physician.

As a boy Wellcome's interest in anthropology was awakened by his observation of the way of life of the American Indians. Here were people whose life-style was totally different from his own, and in many ways admirable to him. The romance of a nomadic, tribal existence, so different from his own career, exerted a powerful influence throughout his life. His passion for travel and love of outdoor activities, his welfare work in Africa and among the American Indians, and his collecting, were all part of this strain of idealism in his character, complementing his business acumen and his devotion to scientific progress.

Even before Wellcome settled in England in 1880 he had made a sufficient collection to be worthy of exhibition. A letter written in 1880 by a friend at his former employer's, Caswell Hazard & Co. of New York, refers to entertainment provided for the American Medical Convention which included 'the finest display at the Hall; your curiosities attracted the most attention from the visiting physicians; the first thing when they entered the room they would notice your collection'. In a letter to Burroughs in 1882 he describes the house he has rented in London: 'All in it is very cheerful; I brought my library and museum from America last winter.'

So Wellcome collected for his own interest and pleasure as a young man. But from 1896 onward there is evidence of a more serious intention, for it was then that he began employing Dr C. J. S. Thompson to do research into the history of medicine and also to acquire objects. One of the first purchases he made for Wellcome was in December 1897 – a book of 'Receits of Phisick and Chirurgery' dated 1692, which cost the remarkably low sum of £2 10s. The following year Thompson joined the staff of Burroughs Wellcome & Co., with whom he remained until 1925 when he retired as Curator of the Wellcome Historical Medical Museum.

During the years of his marriage Wellcome travelled extensively in western Europe, spending many months in France, Spain, Portugal and Madeira. While abroad his main activity was buying for his collection, with a typically single-minded enthusiasm unfortunately not shared by his wife. Syrie Wellcome wrote in 1910: 'Ever since our marriage, the greater part of our time has been spent, as he well knows, in places I detested, collecting curios . . . sacrificing myself in a way I hated, both to please him and gather curios.'

The period up to the First World War was the time when Wellcome did most of his personal collecting, as well as beginning to set up the network of agents buying on his behalf. After the war ended the museum became his primary interest and acquisition was conducted on a business scale under his direction. Wherever he happened to be, even when he was in the Sudan on one of his archaeological expeditions, sale catalogues and museum reports were sent to him. When he was in London, daily briefings always took place on the limits for bidding at auctions. His experienced agents abroad were given a fairly free hand, but they were expected to send detailed reports and it was Wellcome who made all the final decisions to buy or not to buy. The whole operation combined somewhat oddly the excitement of a treasure hunt with efficient business methods.

The satisfaction Wellcome derived from the actual collecting was, however, matched by his pleasure at the interest of the public, and particularly the medical profession, in the series of exhibitions he arranged. These, as he must have realized, helped to secure his acceptance by the world of medicine and science, to which he had no professional entry. The fame of his museum, and his skilful publicizing of it, together with the important research being carried out in the Wellcome laboratories, certainly helped to bring him, late in life, the honours from the world of learning which he coveted.

But for Wellcome the idealist, personal satisfaction was never the main impulse to action. As his evidence to the Royal Commission on National Museums and Galleries made clear, he believed most profoundly in the importance of the influence of the past on the present, and therefore in the educational value of museum collections. He said:

> For the collections of my historical museum I have been gathering material all my life . . . I want to conserve antique objects, and as far as possible to trace each step from the period of their origin throughout the whole course of development . . . I wish something could be done in regard to rare ethnographical materials, also in regard to British works of art, manuscripts and other precious historical things, to prevent them from being taken abroad. So many of the historical treasures of England are now going abroad every year.

Perhaps because of his own origins in a pioneer community, Henry Wellcome believed most profoundly in the value of roots and traditions, not only in the nostalgic sense but as an actual and positive spur to progress.

A Museum of Man in the Making

Henry Wellcome's collection grew steadily during the first thirty-five years of the present century. This was a period when there were few rival collections of this type of material and when, due to the disruption of the First World War, many people were anxious to realize money on their possessions. Even allowing for the change in the value of money, the prices Wellcome paid for many of his purchases seem to us extraordinarily low. It has been estimated that he spent about £400 000 on books and museum objects, making his collection comparable in its field – as he told the Royal Commission – only to the Pitt Rivers Museum in Oxford and the Horniman Museum in London, among private collections.

It is most interesting to trace in the Wellcome records the day-to-day, ant-like activity which built up this vast collection. The central, directing figure is Wellcome himself, with Thompson as his chief assistant. At the turn of the century, when buying started in earnest, the first targets were the leading British auction rooms, and these continued to be regularly visited throughout the next thirty years. In Thompson's reports on acquisitions, the same names regularly occur: Christie's; Stevens's; Sotheby's; Puttick & Simpson's; Hodgson's; Knight, Frank & Rutley's. Wellcome himself seldom attended sales and he tried to keep his extensive buying secret by every possible means. He never used dealers to bid for him, but employed junior members of his staff who kept careful notebooks – many still in the archives – of what they bought and how much was paid for each item. They were given sums in cash to cover what they spent. Pseudonyms were used on all records and goods were collected in a discreetly unidentifiable van. But it was all to no purpose, for the London dealers inevitably found out what was happening, and certainly some mixed lots were made up round items which would catch Wellcome's eye, while there may have been some faking of the 'medical' pictures he bought in large numbers. Gradually a network of agents was built up abroad, so that more and more items are recorded as coming from dealers in Paris, Brussels, Vienna, and indeed all over Europe.

But buying within the trade was not the way to secure the best bargains. As already described, Wellcome himself bought from shops, markets and private individuals when travelling, and he made sure that this type of buying was also carried out by his best-qualified assistants. Thompson made buying trips all over England, and also travelled in Europe and further afield. Just before the First World War he visited Constantinople,having made careful preparations. On 1 January 1914 he reported to Wellcome: 'Letter received from Sir Edwin Peers. He thinks that with the introduction I shall have with me there will be no difficulty in getting access to the libraries and to any objects of interest in the museums in Constantinople.'

In the 1920s a new, dashing figure made his appearance in the Wellcome entourage. Captain P. Johnston-Saint is remembered by surviving colleagues as a man used to the best society, much travelled and a good linguist, the driver of a series of sporting cars. His many contacts abroad, especially in Spain, made him extremely useful to Wellcome and he became a permanent member of the museum staff. He obviously realized how much Wellcome liked to be kept in close touch with his agents abroad and wrote long accounts of his travels.

In 1928 he made a buying tour in northern France and the spring saw him in Paris, spending his days among the stalls by the Seine or visiting medical men and owners of collections. He went to the 'fine old house, 7 rue Clauzel, Montmartre', which housed the medical collection of Dr Noel Hamonic, then in the possession of his two sons. Johnston-Saint reported: 'the collection seems to me to be uncared-for, very dusty and dirty, and no arrangement whatsoever'. The collection was bought for £5000 later in the year. In August Johnston-Saint made a tour of Brittany, where he found the local clergy to be a useful source of information in the search for antiques. He wrote to Wellcome:

> I called on the Curé of St Brieuc and had a long chat with him, and gradually got on to the subject of saints. Many of these curés have widely divergent ideas regarding their statues, and it was necessary to find out what this Curé's ideas were before I could tell him of my object. Fortunately he took a broad view of things, and at last told me where I could get a small statue of St Livertin in carved wood – about 16th century – holding his head between his hands, and widely invoked for pains in the head. He also told me where I could get a typical Breton saint peculiar to this district and who was invoked for heart trouble (the C. was very difficult to understand, speaking a very peculiar French, but I think he meant heart trouble). The name of this saint was St Carabec.
>
> These two saints belonged to an old woman who kept a furniture shop, so I went off there and found them. I bought the two for 440 francs (£3 10s) a price which so astonished me that I hadn't the heart to offer her less.

Statues of saints believed to have the power to cure certain diseases are to be found in considerable numbers in the Wellcome collection.

Johnston-Saint also bought for Wellcome in Spain, and paid visits to Italy, where he kept in contact with Dr Carlo Rossi, who was an agent for Wellcome from 1919 till his death in 1935. Rossi first appears in the correspondence in May 1919, when he was trying to buy an old pharmacy. He corresponded regularly with Thompson at this time, and in 1920 Thompson wrote to him: 'Do you know if Evan Gorga has disposed of his collection of medical objects? He had a few things there I should like to have. Would you have any chance of getting them privately, not mentioning my name?' Wellcome had been on the trail of Gorga's collection ever since 1913, when he had attempted to borrow certain items from it for an exhibition. It was not until 1924 that Gorga's medical collection was finally bought by Wellcome for £8000. But then there was the problem of getting it over to England. During 1924 an extensive search took place for a storeroom in which the collection could be housed in Milan. It had still not left Italy by 1927 when it proved very difficult to get it out of the country because of the Fascist clampdown on exports. Rossi reported that an export permit plus '25% ad valorem export tax' would be needed, 'the value being determined by the authorities'. There are also letters in the file describing problems over missing cases and breakages. The Gorga story demonstrates the amount of patience and administrative effort that was required in assembling Wellcome's collection.

Rossi, like most of Wellcome's foreign agents, was paid on a commission plus expenses basis. Wellcome expected his agents to work very hard for him, and in particular he required regular and detailed reports on what they were up to. They were always finding themselves in the position of asking for more money. Rossi wrote in 1922 to Thompson: 'It is possible here to take a season ticket for the railways fairly cheaply. During the summer I am going to take one for three months on the Rome–Arezzo line. With a little more money, one would be able to take a season ticket for the whole of central Italy, and I should be able to look out for plenty of things for the museum.'

Some of Wellcome's agents were scholars in their own right, like Miss Winifred Blackman of Oxford. She was a qualified anthropologist and started to work for the museum in 1926 on the recommendation of Henry Balfour of the Pitt Rivers. She was paid a retainer per season, together with the cost of any item which she bought. For five years, she made very considerable additions to the collection in the form of Egyptian antiquities.

To find someone capable of buying for the museum in the Far East was by no means easy. In November 1909, Thompson reported on an application for appointment to the staff from a Dr Paira Mall:

He is 33 years of age and has had rather a remarkable career. He is of Hindoo extraction, and was brought up by an English lady with the object of becoming a missionary, being educated for that purpose at Harley College. He preferred medicine, however, and went to Munich, where he took his MD degree at the University, after which he obtained a post as Resident Physician at Fischer's Sanatorium on Lake Constance. From thence, he went to India to take up the appointment of chief medical advisor to the Maharajah of Kapurthala, where he had charge of the Indian Hospitals and five Dispensaries, and superintended the plague operations and inoculations of serum. He then served as army surgeon in the first Japanese army in the Russo–Japanese war, and afterwards returned to Kapurthala for a year and a half, but resigned his post in order to come to England to take his LRCP.

He states he has a great faculty for languages and speaks and writes German, French, Italian, Sanskrit, Persian, Hindustani, Punjabi, Arabic and some Japanese. The salary he asks is from £250–300 a year . . . He said that to his knowledge there was a great mass of manuscripts in the libraries of the Rajahs and in the temples of India, which might yield important results, and his knowledge of Sanskrit would enable him to translate these. I spoke to him also of the oriental Mss in the English Universities, and he said he would be quite capable of making translations, and his knowledge of medicine would prove of great service in making any researches in Mss of an historical medical nature.

Mall was appointed and began work by making translations of early Persian medical manuscripts in the India Office library. He then made several trips to India on behalf of the Museum. He was responsible for buying much of the material in the Oriental Room of the Wellcome Library as well as objects.

The acquisition of notable collections obviously figures most prominently in the museum archives. As well as the Gorga and Hamonic collections already mentioned, one of special interest is that connected with Jenner, the discoverer of vaccination. The Jenner relics first came to Wellcome's notice when arrangements were being made to exhibit them at Cardiff in 1896 to mark the centenary of Jenner's discovery. The collection, belonging to Frederick Mockler, included the original manuscript of Jenner's 'An Inquiry on the Natural History of a Disease known in the Western Counties of England, particularly Glostershire, by the name of Cow Pox', dated Berkeley, 10 July 1797. Wellcome hoped to buy the relics in 1896, but was unsuccessful. In 1903 Mockler was again approached but, by this time in financial embarrassment, he had sold his collection to a Danish engineer, Mikael Pedersen, who lived near him. After prolonged negotiations, Pedersen finally sold the Jenner collection to Thompson for £500 in 1911.

Material relating to Lord Lister, the pioneer of antiseptic surgery, was obviously a coveted addition to an historical medical collection. A few items relating to Lister had been acquired by Wellcome from 1908 onwards, but in 1926 Captain Johnston-Saint went to Scotland with the intention of searching for Lister relics. He was able to buy furniture and fittings from the original Lister ward from a contractor doing demolition work at the Glasgow Royal Infirmary. Further additions were made in the form of gifts of fittings, instruments and photographs from medical men who had worked with Lister. The collection was also augmented by extensive loans from Lister's family, friends and colleagues, and from learned societies. In 1927 the American College

The reconstruction of the Lister Ward, prepared for the Museum in 1926.

of Surgeons celebrated Lister's centenary in Detroit and Wellcome had much of his Lister collection replicated and presented to the College for display on this occasion, while the collection itself was exhibited in his own Museum in Wigmore Street.

Between 1929 and 1931 Wellcome was negotiating through his agents for the purchase of an important French collection of amulets, coins and medical tokens. In December 1929 Mr A. D. Lacaille, one of Wellcome's agents, reported on the collection, and in 1930 Captain Johnston-Saint visited the two rooms at 154 rue de Talbiac, Paris, where Adrien Mortillet had lived almost as a hermit, cataloguing in long-hand his collection of over 20 000 objects. In 1931 Lacaille was in Paris, photographing the collection under a fire of instructions from Wellcome. Eventually the collection was bought for about £1500.

At the other end of the scale of magnitude are the innumerable small purchases made from private individuals, institutions or dealers. Here are some typical examples:

From Bethlehem Hospital: a pair of ancient shackles,

and a pair of handcuffs used in the 18th century for chaining up a violent lunatic: 9s 6d.

From Mrs Helesdon, Andover, wife of the medical practitioner: bell mortars, weighing nearly 30 lbs and bearing the remains of an inscription and dated 1659. Four pairs of primitive midwifery forceps entirely covered with leather. Four old dental keys. One lithotomy forceps, 17th century. One extractor, 17th century. One lithotomy knife, 17th century. A curious dental instrument for extracting teeth. An ancient curved amputating knife with a carved wooden handle. Inclusive price for the above items: £2 10s.

Purchased in the East End of London – an amulet necklace that had belonged to an old Jewess. Composed chiefly of old jet beads, and strung with them numerous amulets, one of metal bearing on it in Hebrew characters a prayer to Jehovah against sterility, and others in the form of hands. Stated that the necklace was worn for a time by each child, and after the child had recovered from a complaint, a lamb bone hand was placed on the necklace to prevent the illness returning: £1.

From curio shops in Rome: a pocket case in red morocco, early 18th century, of silver and tortoise-shell mounted surgical instruments, with the initials and monogram of a doctor in gold on the outside: £1 8s. A small mortar and three old books on magic, surgery and arithmetic, 16th century: £1 17s 4d. Nine engravings of operation scenes . . .: £4 18s 5d.

Knocker from front door of house in Herne Hill where Ruskin was born, purchased from 'the people demolishing the house': £1.

At Exeter from old surgical instrument maker: a good parcel of old midwifery and other instruments: 16s. Also an old fitted inlaid medicine chest, opening back and front: £1.

Mention should be made of Wellcome's particular interest in old pharmacies, which formed so strong a

Imaginary reconstruction of the shop of a seventeenth century apothecary. Formerly in the Wellcome Historical Medical Museum, London, 1913.

link between his study of the history of medicine and his business interests. Five superb reconstructed pharmacies are on show in the entrance hall of the Wellcome building in Euston Road. These are: John Bell's Pharmacy, Oxford Street, London, *circa* 1820; an Hispano–Mauresque pharmacy, *circa* 1790; an Italian pharmacy, 17th century; an English pharmacy, *circa* 1680; and an Arab pharmacy.

The idea of acquiring old furnishings and equipment for reconstruction is typical of Wellcome's style of exhibiting historical material, which has a very strong element of showmanship. The businessman whose display stands startled doctors, pharmacists and the public at the end of last century – who but Wellcome would have introduced a tank of live cod and a sheep to a meeting of the British Medical Association? – knew how effectively historical objects could be combined in three-dimensional reconstructions of actual rooms. With this in mind, he often bought furniture and fittings, unusual items for the collector, in order to show how a hospital ward, a sick room, a consulting room or a pharmacy actually looked in past ages. For the seventeenth century Italian pharmacy he used as his model the pharmacy of the famous Hospital of Santo Spirito in Rome. His efforts to purchase this in the 1920s through Dr Carlo Rossi were unsuccessful, so he bought elsewhere and assembled similar fittings, furniture and equipment. With the Spanish pharmacy he was more lucky, since he acquired the woodwork and contents of the Pontes pharmacy in Granada in 1928. The seventeenth century English pharmacy is again a reconstruction from different sources, but John Bell's pharmacy, founded in Oxford Street, London, in 1798, was actually spotted in course of demolition by Thompson in December 1908 and promptly acquired.

The purchase of items was by no means the sum total of the Wellcome collecting activities. Photographing objects and manuscripts went on all the time. In October 1904 Thompson reported on the discovery, with Dr Louis Sambon, of some very fine drawings at the Bibliothèque Nationale in Paris. He wrote: 'During the month we have gone through 2000 manuscripts altogether, and there remain about another 4000 chiefly early French and Italian to be done, besides the other libraries in Paris and the museums.' The report goes on to say that in the month seventy-two photographs had been taken by Dr Sambon, and arrangements made for the copying of the pictures in the Bibliothèque Nationale by 'two of the ladies who have worked for me at the British Museum'. Sambon was an expert on tropical medicine, who worked for Wellcome for a time. In 1909 research is reported in the libraries in Vienna and Munich. Again, manuscripts were photographed in Munich and over 150 photographs were taken.

The Wellcome collection of medical paintings includes a considerable number of copies, which he commissioned when it was impossible to acquire the original work of art. He also had copies made of statues and other examples of carving, if he was unable to buy the original.

In July 1917 Thompson reported on the sale of the Hope Collection of classical antiquities at Christie's. On the second day of the sale, a statue of the god of health, Asklepios, was bought by Mr Selfridge for 1700 guineas, with Thompson as runner-up in the bidding. So, the following month, an approach was made to Mr Selfridge by the Wellcome museum to allow the statue to be copied. Arrangements were then made with Brucciani's to produce a cast of it for the sum of £140. The Wellcome collection also includes many reproductions of Egyptian friezes dealing with such subjects as the laying out of the dead and embalming.

During Wellcome's lifetime, the acquisition of material for the collection never slackened. Conserving, cataloguing and displaying what was bought took second place, only achieving prominence when an exhibition was planned for some particular occasion. Thus, with the 1913 exhibition in mind, Thompson reported in March 1911 that a start had been made on 'the first classification of the objects for H.M.E. (Historical Medical Exhibition)'. The upper and lower floors at Wigmore Street were lined with trestles and benches and Dr Sambon began identifying the surgical instruments. Later we are told that Dr Sambon was labelling each item ready for mounting on a card, and that nearly all the cases of surgical instruments had been unpacked. But immediately after the burst of activity around 1913 came the war, causing serious disruption to Wellcome's plans. He told the Royal Commission in 1928: 'With only one exception, all my staff, who have been training for years in my work, and carrying out for me researches in the museums and libraries of Europe, entered military service and none returned. During the War the Museum was used for illustrating military surgery. Since then the reorganizing and recruiting of a new staff has taken much time.' Staff problems, frequent moves, and other claims on Wellcome's time and attention, but above all the steady flow of new acquisitions, resulted in the Wellcome Historical Medical Museum never exhibiting during Wellcome's lifetime, as he himself said, 'more than one-tenth of my collections'. The rest of the material remained in packing cases and no comprehensive catalogue was ever made.

The Historical Medical Collection

If a precise date has to be sought for the birth of the Wellcome Historical Medical Collection, it would almost certainly be 1898, when Dr C. J. S. Thompson became a member of the firm's staff to work on medical history. It is interesting to note that in addition to augmenting the Wellcome Collection and preparing it for exhibition Thompson was responsible for a succession of booklets on the history of medicine produced as advertising material by Burroughs Wellcome & Co., usually to coincide with a medical congress. The titles include: *Oxford Medical Lore* (1905); *Anaesthetics, Ancient and Modern* (1907); *The Evolution of Antiseptic Surgery* (1910); and *The Dental Art in Ancient Times* (1914). As Wellcome, that astute advertiser, clearly saw, the appeal of such material, attractively presented to groups of medical men, could not fail to increase his firm's reputation. To return to the collection, it is clear that the systematic amassing of material for the purpose of exhibition really began with Thompson's appointment, and as early as 1905, the occasion of his firm's twenty-fifth anniversary, Wellcome hoped to present a historical medical exhibition in London. The preparations, however, could not be completed in time, for Wellcome's plans were always on a grand scale. By 1912, following a world-wide appeal for material connected with the history of medicine, he was able to announce: 'The preparations are now so far advanced that I have decided to hold the exhibition in London in the year 1913, at the time of the meeting of the International Medical Congress in this city.'

The spur of a target date led to a fever of activity, the more so because there was a considerable response to the appeal for material. Gifts as well as loans poured in, and many of the items originally lent for the 1913 exhibition were subsequently bought by Wellcome.

On 24 June 1913 the exhibition was formally opened at the Wellcome Historical Medical Museum in 54a Wigmore Street by Sir Norman Moore, President of the Section of History of Medicine at the 17th International Congress of Medicine. Wellcome had the title of Director of the Museum, and Thompson was appointed Curator. His special interests were pharmacy and toxicology, and he wrote several books on the history of these subjects. He was largely responsible for acquiring the Lister material for the Museum.

After the war, despite loss of staff and other setbacks, the Museum was opened for a series of congresses, and for lectures and meetings, as well as visits by distinguished people, though frequent periods of closure intervened. Wellcome was far from satisfied throughout the 1920s with the location and scale of his Museum, and stated that he only allowed it to open because of popular demand. Yet his notable gift for publicity caused the reputation of his collection to grow steadily, and brought a two-fold gain. On the one hand, its reputation brought gifts, loans and information on the whereabouts of suitable material for the collection. On the other, Wellcome became increasingly accepted in the medical world on the strength of the value of his exhibitions to medicine.

As Wellcome's projects outside his business grew in importance and in size, the need for a building to house them became of pressing importance. During the late 1920s various sites were considered. Wellcome finally decided upon one in Euston Road which included the buildings of the Bureau of Scientific Research and the Museum of Medical Science. The Museum was dismantled and stored at the Imperial Institute, temporary premises were found for the Bureau in Kilburn, and the site was cleared during 1930. The architect, Septimus Warwick, designed a dignified, classical building, and

A view of the Wellcome Building, 183 Euston Road.

its foundation stone was laid by the President of the Royal College of Surgeons on 25 November 1931. Wellcome's intention was that it should house his research laboratories and museums, to be collectively known as the Wellcome Research Institution.

By 1932 the Wellcome Building in Euston Road was ready for occupation, and the Bureau of Scientific Research, the Chemical Research Laboratories, the Museum of Medical Science and the Historical Medical Museum were moved into it. The latter museum remained closed, however, in order to undergo complete replanning. Also intended to find a home on the Euston Road site, but in a different building, was Wellcome's Library, which he saw as a research aid to the entire Institution. Four years later came Wellcome's death, and the Historical Medical Museum and the Library were still largely in store.

The thirty years between 1937 and 1967, when plans to find a home for the Historical Medical Museum in a national museum were first discussed, were a period of sustained effort to bring some order to the massive collections of objects and books amassed by Wellcome. The sort of difficulty faced by his museum staff in the last years of his life is indicated in a letter he sent from Washington to Mr L. W. G. Malcolm, the conservator, on 4 July 1933. Wellcome wrote:

> I would remind you that at the time I began arranging for the removal of the W.H.M.M., from Wigmore Street to the new building, I took you, together with Captain Saint and Mr Port through all my storehouses containing my extensive collections made over a period of many years for the W.H.M.M. and I explained to you explicitly what I wanted first of all – all my ethnological, anthropological, archaeological and all other primitive material sorted out, classified, prepared, numbered and catalogued. Also, I gave you definite instructions that these materials must be sorted, classified and grouped scientifically so as to facilitate the final arrangement of the materials in the prehistoric and primitive halls.
>
> Furthermore, I told you that I would personally supervise and direct the arrangement of these exhibits and decide the methods of display of all the afore-mentioned materials.

In the letter, Wellcome rebuked Malcolm for using his own initiative in getting on with arranging some of the prehistoric material. Wellcome's refusal to delegate, combined with his increasing ill-health and the pressure of other work, meant that while purchases poured into the storerooms, very little was in fact done to sort out the new material. In 1937 the two men in charge of the Wellcome collections were Captain Johnston-Saint, conservator of the Museum, and S. A. Moorat, the librarian; both reported bi-monthly on work in their departments. In November 1938, Johnston-Saint wrote: 'A start has been made in opening up cases which arrived in this country some ten or twelve years ago, having been shipped here from America and elsewhere by Sir Henry Wellcome.' The Museum store, then at Hythe Road, Willesden, was piled high with cases whose contents were as varied as they were daunting. In May 1939 Johnston-Saint reported that the arms and weapons collection at Willesden was being sorted out, but that 'some more zoological specimens have been unpacked, which include about a dozen crocodiles of various sizes and some stuffed snakes'. The necessity to close the Museum following the outbreak of war came as a relief, since it gave uninterrupted opportunity to get on with cataloguing and research.

The librarian was facing similar problems. In June 1938 Mr Moorat reported that he himself had first become involved with the Library in 1923. In the period between that date and Wellcome's death in 1936, he wrote that 'extensive purchases of books from all sources and on every subject on a scale greater than ever before' had been made. In a book store at Stratford Mews, 20 000 books were on the shelves and many

Original packing cases and other items in the Museum store.

more piled in the bundles in which they had come from the auctions. During Wellcome's life there were strict instructions that no book should be disposed of in any way, even though the collection included considerable numbers of paperback novels and modern reprints.

During the war years the work of sorting, classifying and disposal of completely non-relevant material continued in both Museum and Library, despite staff shortages – Johnston-Saint reported losing sixteen staff to the armed forces – and some damage and disruption caused by enemy action. Even greater problems, however, resulted from changes of plan over the use of the building at Euston Road. In 1937 Johnston-Saint had produced a plan for the layout of the Historical Medical Museum on three floors at Euston Road and this was followed by a revised plan described in March 1941 by Dr S. A. Daukes, newly appointed as director both of the Historical Medical Collection and the Museum of Medical Science. The latter plan was to create a permanent chronological exhibition in nine halls, each measuring 110 × 40 ft, and a hall of statuary. Neither of these plans was able to be realised because of claims on the available space both by the Library, which was moved into Euston Road late in 1941, and by the administrative offices of the Wellcome Foundation, which were bombed out at Snow Hill. The final result was that in 1948 the Historical Medical Museum was effectively transferred to 53 Portman Square, though some exhibitions were still held at Euston Road. Staff changes coincided with the end of the war. Dr E. Ashworth Underwood was appointed in January 1946 as director of the Museum and Library, in succession to Dr Daukes, and Mr Moorat retired in the same year, to be succeeded as librarian by Mr W. J. Bishop. In April 1946 Dr Underwood reported the death of Mr A. W. Haggis, who had been in charge of the Museum's official publications, as well as working on the medieval medicine collection. Captain Johnston-Saint also seems to have left the Museum in the late 1940s, as his name

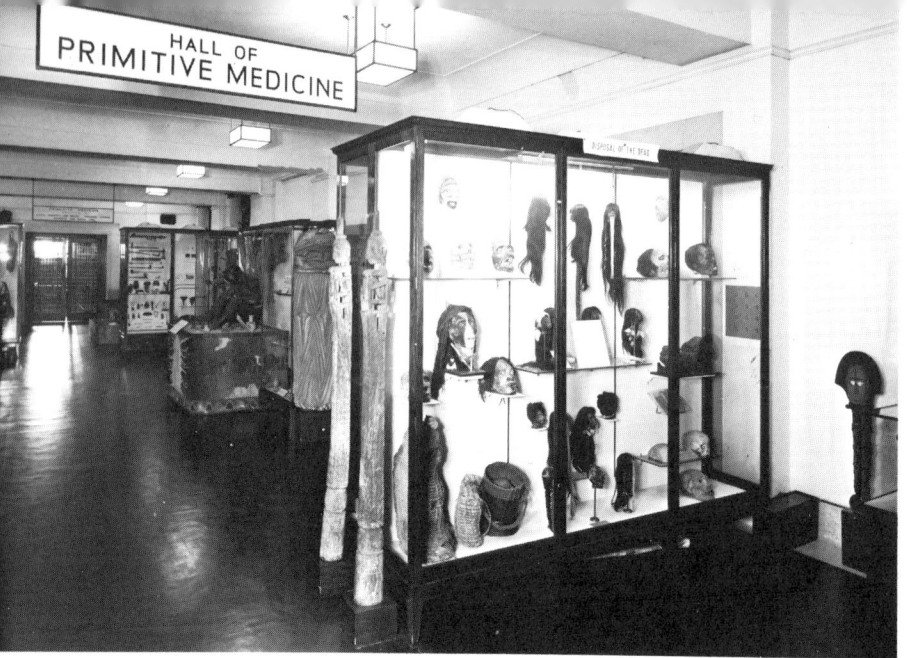

Part of the Museum in the 1940s.

ceases to appear in the reports. But Mr A. D. Lacaille, an archaeologist who had acted as a buying agent for Wellcome as early as 1929, continued to work on the Museum's ethnographic and prehistoric collections until he retired in 1959. His book, *The Stone Age in Scotland*, was published in 1954 by the Oxford University Press.

Dr Underwood, who served as director of the Museum and Library until 1964, came to the post from a career in public health. He was an honorary lecturer and later research fellow in the history and philosophy of science at University College, London, and achieved an international reputation as a historian of medicine. His major publication was the *History of the Society of Apothecaries of London*. His bi-monthly reports on the Museum and Library reveal his determined efforts to carry out Wellcome's intentions for his collection. Qualified staff continued to unpack, examine and catalogue material, but seemed to make little impression on its vastness. In 1949, when the packing cases suffered one of their periodic transfers, '59 vanloads' were moved. It had become clear that Wellcome's vast concept of a museum of man would never be realised; the Wellcome Historical Medical Museum would have to be limited to the subject contained in its title. So other museums were invited to examine groups of non-medical objects with a view to accepting them as gifts or loans. In this way the bulk of the Stone Age and ethnographic collections were given to the British Museum and, at a later date, what remained was placed on permanent loan to the University of California. Other, smaller groups of objects went to other institutions. While the work of examining and sorting continued, a sequence of exhibitions was mounted, either at Portman Square or at Euston Road. Notable exhibitions during Dr Underwood's directorship included: 'The Jenner Centenary Exhibition', 'Medicine in 1850', 'Prehistoric Man in Health and Sickness', 'The Life and Work of Henry Wellcome', 'Medicine Under Three Queens: Elizabeth, Anne and Victoria', 'The Ehrlich Centenary Exhibition' and 'Electricity in the Service of Medicine'.

In 1957 the store was moved again, to Dartford. Here Underwood experienced constant problems over the condition of the warehouses, which proved not to be weatherproof. He was also very worried about the lack of gallery space, even after the Museum moved back to Euston Road from Portman Square in 1954. In January 1958 he wrote: 'The gallery space for such a vast and important collection is ludicrously small . . . I am convinced that very soon consideration will have to be given to the problem of providing adequate accommodation for the Museum and Library.' Yet the number of visitors increased steadily, from just over 1000 a year in 1950 to 7000 in 1964.

Dr Underwood was succeeded as director in 1964 by Dr F. N. L. Poynter. Having joined the staff of the Wellcome Library in 1930, at the age of 22, Noel Poynter devoted his entire working life to the Wellcome collection, retiring in 1973. From the time when he was commended for his efforts in moving library books to safety in the basement at Euston Road during the blitz,

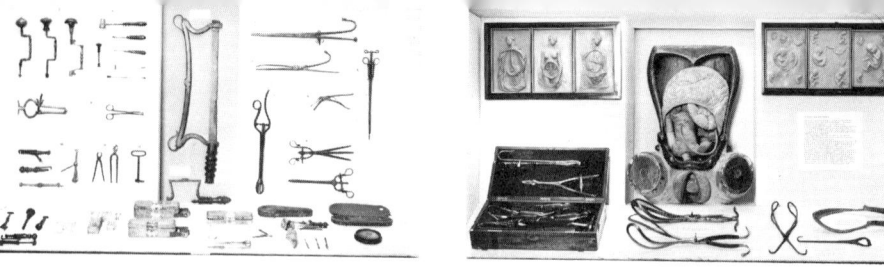
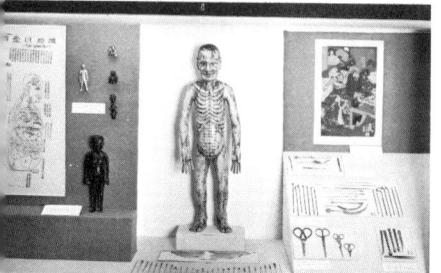

Museum showcases from the 1960s: (a) *Surgical instruments,* (b) *obstetrics,* (c) *acupuncture,* (d) *ethnography.*

his energy was unflagging in the organization and promotion of the two institutions under his care. As a librarian, the Library came first with him; he was the driving force behind the publication of Moorat's catalogue of the Wellcome manuscript collection and in 1954 he himself published a *Catalogue of Incunabula in the Wellcome Historical Medical Library.* He, like Underwood, was harassed by lack of space. He wrote in 1959: 'Offers of many hundreds of useful volumes, many of which will have to be bought at some future date to avoid serious gaps, have had to be refused for want of accommodation.' Later he commented that the Library had 'lost 25% of space in the Wellcome building, though it had acquired 25 000 books in ten years.'

At the start of Poynter's directorship there was only one gallery available, where an exhibition on 'Medicine in Shakespeare's England', which attracted over 18 000 visitors, was mounted in 1965. While he was in charge, Dr Poynter was able to realize his intention to establish a permanent history of medicine display on the first and second floors of the Wellcome building, which were

New cases in the Museum store, introduced under Dr Poynter.

released for expansion of the museum exhibition. On the first floor, a consecutive display of medicine in different ages was mounted, as well as a specialist exhibition on the history of ophthalmology. A gallery on the second floor was used for special exhibitions, including one on medicine in war. Dr Poynter also devoted his energy to getting the stored museum material finally sorted and properly arranged. In 1965 he wrote: 'With the clearance from the stores of a great quantity of irrelevant material, it has been possible to gain a much clearer idea of the size and scope of the specifically medical collections.' Two thousand new containers were acquired, shelving was installed, and additional expert staff were recruited to work on the collection. These included Mr J. W. Barber-Lomax, who catalogued the Graeco–Roman surgical instruments, and Dr J. K. Crellin, who published a *Catalogue of Medical Ceramics: Vol. I, English and Dutch.*

Dr Poynter was active internationally in the fields of bibliography and history of medicine. He was secretary and later president of the International Academy of the History of Medicine, and presided over its international congress in London in 1972. He edited the quarterly journal *Medical History* from 1964 to 1973, and introduced the quarterly bibliography *Current Work in the History of Medicine*, invaluable to medical historians. He established the Wellcome Institute and Library as internationally important centres for the study of the history of medicine and made them responsible for the publication of an extensive monograph series.

In 1967 the Trustees arranged an international symposium to help them decide on future policy in the history of medicine. As a result of the recommendations of this symposium, a smaller panel of scholars was appointed to advise the Trustees on a regular basis. In 1972 this panel recommended that the Wellcome Institute should develop as a postgraduate centre for research into the history of medicine. It should therefore be strengthened academically by the appointment of further staff and the Library developed as an international research facility. This left the Museum static and largely in store, an unsatisfactory state of affairs which, the panel suggested, could be remedied by arranging for it to be transferred in some way to one of the national museums.

The obvious national institution was the Science Museum, London, which was duly approached in the early 1970s. The negotiations involved seeking a legal ruling on whether the Trustees could, under the terms of Wellcome's will, make the collection over to the Science Museum on permanent loan. The Charity Commissioners were not prepared to give a decision, but the Appeal Court agreed to the transfer on the

Science Museum accepting certain special conditions to safeguard the collection in accordance with the wishes of Henry Wellcome.

In July 1976 the transfer of the Wellcome Historical Medical Collection to the Science Museum on permanent loan was publicly announced. In April 1977 the first Keeper of the Wellcome Museum of the History of Medicine in the Science Museum took up his post. The task facing the staff was, and still is, a formidable one. Until the work of cataloguing the entire collection in store is completed no one can say how many objects it comprises, since the existing records are quite inadequate. By December 1979 the first 30 000 objects had been catalogued. The card catalogue will provide a complete record of the entire Wellcome Collection, and will of course be available to scholars for research. The information will also be put on computer retrieval.

While cataloguing is in progress every object is inspected to decide its relevance to the history of medicine. If an object is not strictly medical in its own right, it may still be found a place in the Wellcome Museum for the History of Medicine on the basis of association, or usefulness as background for the displays. Some objects may be transferred to other Science Museum departments and still others may be disposed of to more appropriate institutions by the Wellcome Trustees. If there is doubt about the significance of an object, outside advice is sought, for the further any object is from us in time or space, the harder it is to be sure of the purpose for which it was intended.

So much for the ordering and cataloguing of this vast collection. The second purpose of the loan, however, is to ensure that the public is able to enjoy and learn from a selection of the objects, as Wellcome intended. The Science Museum, which has more than three million visitors a year viewing its ten acres of public gallery, is an ideal place in which to present an exhibition, always bearing in mind that the large majority of visitors are non-specialists. Two galleries have been built to exhibit

Diorama prepared for the lower gallery of the Wellcome Museum of the History of Medicine at the Science Museum: Victorian delivery scene.

the Wellcome Museum. The aim of the lower gallery is to offer glimpses of the development of medical history in such a way that the schoolchild, student or lay adult can identify with the subject. It is difficult to understand the cultural background which gives immense power to a witch doctor or led the Egyptians to use certain remedies in ancient times. So this introductory gallery illustrates the evolution of modern medicine by putting the past and the present side by side. Lister's surgical ward contrasts with a modern operating theatre; dentists' surgeries of 1890, 1930 and 1980 can be compared. Where the actual objects are to hand, the scenes are full-scale reconstructions in the true Wellcome tradition. Naturally, the Science Museum has acquired some modern surgical and dental equipment. Where the real

Diorama, as above: First World War Dressing Station.

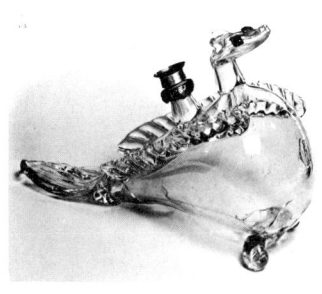
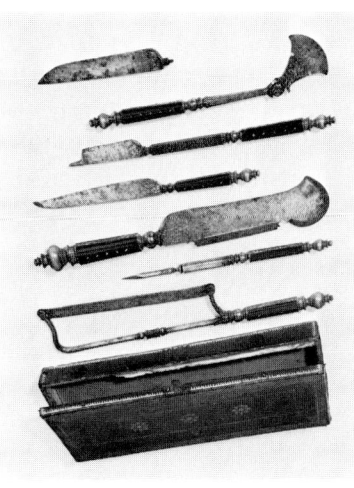
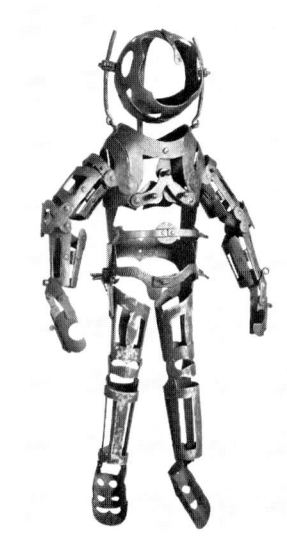

Four single objects from the upper gallery: (a) French eighteenth century drug jar, (b) Seventeenth century Italian infant's feeding bottle, (c) hunting trousse (case of instruments), dated 1570, (d) Sixteenth century iron manikin (anatomical model).

objects are not available, dioramas or models are used very effectively.

The upper gallery, open from 1981, is considerably larger, and shows the historical development of medicine by means of objects, graphics and descriptive labelling. The displays, largely chronological, include a self-contained section of material from non-literate cultures, and from non-Western medicine. Half the space in the gallery, however, is to be devoted to medicine since 1800, emphasizing its scientific basis.

Because so many school parties visit the Science Museum – and also because Wellcome himself was deeply concerned with the educational function of museums – both galleries are specially geared to teaching, and educational packs are provided linking the two displays.

The upper gallery contains much material from the original Wellcome collections and also some later material. The Wellcome Museum in the Science Museum will, like its parent body, continue to acquire material by all possible means, and is always glad to hear of any significant medical objects available as gifts or for purchase. Acquisition is now the responsibility of the Science Museum. As already described, this was one of the factors that led to the transfer of the collection. But the Wellcome Trustees are actively involved in an advisory capacity and through their financial support.

The aim is to have the entire collection accessible to the public as Wellcome would have wished. He saw a museum as having two functions; the popular, which will be fulfilled by the galleries; and the research function, which is catered for, as he was never able to do, by having all the objects available in store and completely catalogued.

Henry Wellcome's Library

Since Wellcome regarded his Library as a service department to his Museum of Man, it is not surprising that he collected books, manuscripts and other printed material from a wider range of subjects than the purely medical. He was concerned with 'the preservation of life and health' in Man, in all ages and cultures. A recent select index to the Library's classification gives some idea of the range of subjects covered, as the following random list shows: advertising, agriculture, astrology, atomic theory, botany, Buddhism, cookery, cosmetics, demo-

The Hall of Statuary of the Museum in the 1930s (now the main reading-room of the Library).

graphy, demonology, embalming, medical ethics, freemasonry, genetics, gymnastics, health education, medical illustration, magnetism, missions, papyri, penicillin, public health, radiology, scientific societies, statistics, trials, weights & measures. To stress the range and variety of the Library, the way in which it provides a cross-section of civilization, is not to belittle its practical usefulness to the modern scholar of medicine and its history and to those from many associated disciplines. All current periodicals in the history of medicine and science are taken, together with a number of others from medical science and general history. New books in the field are purchased as a matter of course; the Library's present policy is to acquire those books which reflect modern scholarly interests in the social relations of medicine in history. Historical demography, the philosophical, ethical, administrative and political aspects of medicine and health may serve as examples.

The period from 1900 to 1930 was, as we now know, the last in which it was possible to buy old books, manuscripts and antique objects relatively cheaply. Some of the prices Wellcome paid seem, indeed, incredibly low. For example, a fourteenth-century medical manuscript, described in the Sotheby catalogue for 3 February 1908 as 'MS. on vellum, 101 11. with some additions in other hands, contemporary binding, oak boards, stamped pigskin', is annotated as costing £7 5s 0d; while £2 5s 0d was paid for a seventeenth-century document entitled 'A Humble Remonstrance addressed to the House of Commons, asking them to appoint and pay a certain number of certified physicians and apothecaries who should devote their exclusive attention to those sick of the Plague'.

In secure storage are the manuscript collection, all books printed before 1850, and collections of correspondence which include letters from Florence Nightingale and documents relating to Lord Nelson, both of whom were concerned with health in the armed forces, and correspondence from leading medical pioneers such as Pasteur, Lister and Jenner.

Of the 14 000 manuscripts in the Wellcome Library, about 1500 date from before 1650, the earliest being an Anglo-Saxon fragment giving remedies for treating lung disease, tumours and so on. The greatest treasure is an early fifteenth-century Apocalypse from the Low German area which contains, in addition to the Revelation, an anatomical section, finely illustrated in colour. The collection of early manuscripts also includes about 40 herbals, and texts on medieval medicine in Latin, English, German, Italian and French. Hand-written material from later centuries includes many lecture notes from British and European medical schools which provide an excellent source of information on the history of medical education. There are also books of remedies, commonplace books, diaries and journals. An interesting example of this last category is the log kept by Denis Gascoigne Lillie, who was a marine biologist with Captain Scott's 1910 expedition to Antarctica. The entire western manuscript collection was catalogued by S. A. Moorat, on his retirement as librarian.

In 1954 Dr Noel Poynter's *Catalogue of Incunabula in the Wellcome Historical Medical Library* was published. It contained descriptions of 632 books printed before 1501, the majority of which were acquired through the purchase of three famous private libraries: those of William Morris (bought in 1898), Dr J. F. Payne (bought in 1911), and Kurt Wolff (bought in 1926). Three further catalogues of the Library were published between 1962 and 1976, describing books printed up to 1850. Among the early treasures in the Library are Andrew Boorde's *Breviary of Health* (1547), Timothy Bright's *Treatise on Melancholy* (1586), which has been associated with Shakespeare's *Hamlet,* and Stephen Bradwell's *Helps for Suddain Accidents* (1633), the earliest first aid manual.

In the Oriental Room are housed over 10 000 items, representing a very wide range of eastern languages. As well as many in Arabic, Sanskrit and Persian, examples exist in Ethiopian, Tibetan, Coptic, Syriac, and others. Much of the material was collected between 1910 and 1926 by Dr Paira Mall, whose appointment to the staff of the Museum has already been described. In this section of the Library are manuscripts in almost bizarre variety, ranging from Arabic and Persian illuminations much in the western style, to strange scripts on palm leaves, metal, leather and wood.

Henry Wellcome's American birth and his early travels in South America caused him to take a special interest in early medical books and documents from the American continent. He bought the important collection of Dr Nicolas Leon, and later the collection of Dr Francisco Guerra was added. Included in the South American collection are the first book on medicine printed in the New World, the *Phisica Speculatio* by Veracruz (1557), and an original document signed by the Count of Chinchon, whose name was given by Linnaeus to cinchona, from which quinine was later isolated. Wellcome's interest in cinchona is shown by his organization of a tercentenary exhibition at the

The main reading room of the Library between 1949 and 1956.

Historical Medical Museum in 1930, to commemorate the discovery of the therapeutic properties of the bark.

A sub-department of the Library, typical of the omnivorous collecting habit of its founder, is the extensive picture collection, the portraits of which have been catalogued by Dr R. Burgess. As well as some extremely interesting oil paintings on medical subjects, this collection includes 12 000 portrait engravings and watercolours, as well as photographs of conferences and lectures, operating scenes, and caricatures. In all, this represents an amazing and most valuable medical and scientific portrait gallery. The collection contains some real curiosities, such as the sequence of twelve large anatomical paintings by the eighteenth-century French engraver, Gautier d'Agoty. Wellcome was prepared to collect what is known as ephemera – printed matter which is considered expendable – long before such things were seriously accepted to be of historical importance. A typical acquisition was: 'Old Apothecaries' and quack doctors' trade cards and circulars, 1914, £4 4s 0d'.

The main reading room of the Library as re-opened in 1974.

Like the bulk of the museum objects, the Library remained in a warehouse, undergoing sorting, until the 1940s, when it was moved to the Wellcome Building in Euston Road. It was opened to readers in 1949, was completely refurnished and modernised in the early 1960s, and was re-opened by Lord Brain in September 1962. It is now part of the Wellcome Institute for the History of Medicine. The Wellcome Building as it now exists was completed in 1931 but is only a part of its founder's design. It was hoped to build a new home for the Library on the Euston Road site, but this was never achieved and the present rooms it occupies were not intended for this purpose.

However, the main reading room has space and good proportions. It is on two levels, with a balcony round all four sides, reached by a wide staircase. There are reading bays divided by jutting bookcases. At the end opposite the stairs is an exhibition platform backed by a screen bearing life-sized enlargements of figures, probably drawn in Titian's studio, to illustrate the great sixteenth-century work by Vesalius on the structure of the human body. Here are the books on open access and some older printed books in glass-fronted cases, available on application to the librarian. The reading room is reached through the catalogue room and the periodicals room, and leading off the gallery are the Oriental and South American collections.

The Wellcome Library contains over 400 000 printed books, 14 000 Western and Oriental manuscripts and 100 000 autograph letters. It is one of the world's great specialist libraries, reaching back into the past with rare manuscripts and first editions, yet offering the latest in new books and journals to the modern student of the history of medicine.

The Museum of Medical Science

Henry Wellcome fully realized the value of museum material in education. An expert in advertising, he knew that striking visual presentations are more easily remembered than the written or spoken word alone. So he gave his full support to an entirely separate museum which came into existence through the medical research he sponsored in the Sudan.

It will be remembered that Wellcome had, in 1901, financed a medical laboratory in the Sudan under the direction of Andrew Balfour. This carried out pioneer work on tropical medicine and hygiene that became world famous through the series of scientific papers published by Wellcome as 'The Reports of the Wellcome Research Laboratories at the Gordon Memorial College, Khartoum' and known more simply as the Khartoum Reports. In 1912 Wellcome handed the entire operation over to the Sudanese government and Balfour returned to London to direct the Wellcome Bureau of Scientific Research in Henrietta Street. Balfour's encouragement led to the establishment of a museum of specimens and illustrative material on tropical diseases, associated with the Bureau. After the First World War, during which the Bureau had been most useful to the government,

The Museum of Medical Science as it was first opened in Henrietta Street, during the First World War.

Wellcome decided to expand the museum and acquired new premises in Vere Street. In June 1919 Dr Sidney Daukes became its Director. He was a pioneer of visual education, which he had used with great success during the war at the Army School of Hygiene. It was his display technique in what was then called the Wellcome Museum of Tropical Medicine and Hygiene which created a teaching resource that has been in constant use for the past sixty years by the medical profession.

In 1923 Balfour's place as Director of the Bureau of Scientific Research was taken by Dr C. M. Wenyon and in the same year the scope of the Museum was widened to cover not simply tropical but also general medicine. Daukes' design was to show, by means of a series of study cubicles containing graphic material and specimens, the latest knowledge on different diseases and the steps by which such knowledge had been reached. In each case cause, prevention and treatment were described under ten headings, colour coded to make easier comparison between the different diseases.

The Museum of Medical Science, now part of the Wellcome Foundation, occupies two galleries in the Wellcome Building in Euston Road. It contains material of great historical interest, which includes original drawings by the great medical illustrator, Amedeo Terzi, and drawings and microscopical preparations by Dr C. M. Wenyon. But it is essentially a modern teaching aid, of great interest to the student of contemporary tropical medicine. Unlike the other medical museums in London, the majority of which are associated with teaching hospitals and concentrate on pathology, the Wellcome Museum of Medical Science has a very broad approach to the study of disease, and the special bias towards tropical complaints which remains is of great value today because so many diseases from tropical countries are being brought to the West as a result of the modern ease of travel.

Although the Museum of Medical Science does not contain material personally collected by Wellcome, and is of a highly specialized type, it provides yet another example of his imaginative support of medical science.

The Special Quality of the Wellcome Collection

Henry Wellcome was essentially a public man, in the sense that he was at his happiest and most effective when dealing with people in large groups rather than as individuals. His collecting followed the same pattern, being geared towards the presentation of exhibitions and the planning of a museum, rather than towards acquiring especially choice items for his own private enjoyment. In fact, he was different in most respects from the connoisseur collector, who deploys great wealth to own single treasures in a limited field. His collecting was all-embracing rather than selective, he made no attempt to develop profound knowledge or taste and his purpose was educative rather than aesthetic.

The Wellcome collection has sometimes been criticized as a hotchpotch, brought together by a man who understood little about what he was buying. It is true that Wellcome was not a scholar or a historian, but he was shrewd, quick to pick up information, and possessed of a most retentive memory. He did not surround himself with experts when working on his collection, as he did with such success in promoting scientific research. Though he employed many assistants, one gets the impression that he wished to keep his museum very much as his own personal creation.

Yet to accuse him of collecting mindlessly is to do him a grave injustice. He knew exactly what he was trying to achieve. He wanted to save from destruction man's past activity and achievement in medicine because he firmly believed that knowledge of the past is the most successful basis for progress in the future. The present, he believed, must respect and learn from the past – knowledge is a tree whose lofty growth depends on deep, sound roots.

What Wellcome attempted was nothing less than the recreation of man's medical past, rather as the archaeologist seeks to recreate from objects the period of prehistory, before there were written records. This was an impressively novel concept, particularly in Wellcome's day, and one of great concern to the museum profession and to historians. The idea of a museum as a three-dimensional book now receives wide acceptance. Wellcome, however, appreciated that a museum must have a dual aspect: education and entertainment for the general public; and material for study and research for the scholar.

If his collecting activity is looked at from this standpoint, the amassing of objects takes on quite a different appearance. An example will clarify the point. The Wellcome collection of microscopes is one of the three largest in the world, numbering around 1500 instruments and parts. Of these only about 100 are important examples in fine condition, including some of the earliest specimens from the late seventeenth and early eighteenth centuries, and instruments of unique importance, such as the prototype achromatic microscope made for J. J. Lister. The rest are instruments, complete and incomplete, which singly are of no great value. But together, in such numbers, they provide important information on the instrument-making trade, giving the names of lesser-known makers and retailers and showing how frequently standard parts were used in different assemblies, signed by different retailers. This information is available not only for English-made microscopes but also for continental ones, which, because of Wellcome's collecting methods, are unusually well-represented. So the fact that Wellcome did not reject incomplete and undistinguished instruments is of great value to the historian of scientific instruments and the same is clearly true throughout the collection. Wellcome said that his purpose was 'to conserve antique objects and as far as possible to trace each step from the period of their origin throughout the whole course of development'.

So a closer examination of his collecting activity reveals Henry Wellcome as a man of remarkable intellectual vision, whose own industry and ability gave him the means to achieve – though only in part – his concept. It is a most happy circumstance that, more than forty years after his death, his dream of a combined educational and research museum of medical history is on the way to becoming true.

Part Three

The Legacy, the Wellcome Trust

Establishment and Early Years

HENRY Wellcome's name for the business and research organization he created in 1924 – the Wellcome Foundation Ltd – has caused some confusion since the Trust bearing his name came into existence under the terms of his will. The reason for this is that the title 'foundation' is more commonly used to describe an endowed charity, for example, The Nuffield Foundation. In this sense it is the Wellcome Trust that is a 'foundation' – hence the confusion.

It is likely that when Wellcome first decided to create a Board of Trustees as sole shareholders of the Foundation under his will, he envisaged them as simply providing for the continuation of his business enterprises and the research laboratories and museums he had created as accessories to the business. He saw these as being so closely related to the business that he included them within the Foundation (a move which later caused certain problems to the Trustees). However, by the time the will was formulated in 1932, it had become clear that after the needs of the business and certain specific bequests were taken care of, there would still be a large residue of income to be disposed of. Wellcome therefore set out in his will the objects for which the Trustees should use these funds:

(1) . . . the advancement of research work bearing upon medicine, surgery, chemistry, physiology, bacteriology, therapeutics, materia-medica, pharmacy

and allied subjects and any subject or subjects which have or at any time may develop importance for scientific research which may conduce to the improvement of the physical conditions of mankind, and in particular for the discovery, invention and improvement of medicinal agents and methods for the prevention and cure of disorders, and the control or extermination of insects and other pests which afflict human beings and animal and plant life in tropical and other regions and elsewhere . . .

(2) . . . the establishment and endowment and future maintenance of any new research Museum or Library and for the purchase and acquisition of books, manuscripts, documents, pictures and other works of art and other objects and things for such research Museums or Libraries and for conducting research and collecting information connected with the history of medicine, surgery, chemistry, bacteriology, pharmacy and allied sciences.

The will explicitly excluded from the objects to which the residual fund might be applied anything not legally charitable.

Five Trustees were appointed under the will. Wellcome specified that two should be qualified in medicine and allied sciences, and two experienced businessmen with knowledge of the law and estate administration. Following Wellcome's death the original Trustees, from 1938 under the chairmanship of Sir Henry Dale, encountered considerable problems of administration and adjustment which were aggravated by the Second World War. The Trustees had to arrange for the appointment of a Board of Directors for the Wellcome Foundation Ltd, which had, until Wellcome's death, been to a large extent under his personal control. The adjustment of the business to a different mode of control was made much slower and more difficult by wartime conditions and in particular by the destruction in January 1941 of the offices at Snow Hill Buildings in the City of London. This meant that part of the business had to be accommodated at Euston Road, with resulting disturbance to the Museum and Library.

The Trustees were also faced with the obligation to pay considerable estate duty based on the value of shares in the business which, it must be remembered, included the Wellcome collection and Library. Both the will and an associated memorandum had made it clear that Wellcome wished the Trustees to be responsible for the Museum and Library, but in formal terms they were assets of the Foundation. This anomalous position had to be cleared up to enable the Trustees to become the legal owners of the Historical Medical Museum and Library, with the Foundation as agents responsible for their housing and administration.

The Trustees also had to deal with specific bequests under the will and with enterprises which Wellcome had set in motion shortly before his death. One bequest that the Trustees immediately concerned themselves with was that which provided for a memorial to Wellcome's parents at Garden City, Minnesota. While he was still alive, Wellcome had acquired a freehold property in Garden City and there he intended to provide a public library, assembly hall, park and sports ground. As funds became available to them the Trustees set aside the $400 000 designated in the will, and at the same time they made enquiries and received reports from local advisers on exactly what form the memorial should take. Garden City had remained the small centre of a scattered rural community, its main feature being a school. It was decided that the memorial fund should provide the school with a library and an assembly hall which could be converted for indoor sports. Any residual funds could be used for Wellcome scholarships to send pupils from the Garden City school to the university. The Wellcome Memorial was opened by Sir Henry Dale in 1959 and handed over to the care of special trustees who were to administer the maintenance grant bequeathed under the will.

While on the subject of Wellcome's association with the land of his birth it is appropriate to mention that a separate foundation for the support of research was created by Burroughs Wellcome Inc. in the USA, called the Burroughs Wellcome Fund. This foundation is independent of the Wellcome Trust, and is based at Research Triangle Park in North Carolina. It supports medical research, mainly in the USA, and has been particularly concerned with the development of clinical pharmacology.

Wellcome's personal interest in two archaeological enterprises in the Middle East was followed through by the Trustees in the early years. At the site where he had personally spent much time, Jebel Moya in the Sudan, the excavations were closed down and remaining material transported home. The Trustees then arranged for research on the project to be completed and published by the Oxford University Press under the title *The Wellcome Excavations in the Sudan*. This consisted of three volumes, two on Jebel Moya and the third on adjoining sites. Wellcome had also given financial support to archaeological work at Lachish in Palestine, and this enterprise too was brought to a proper conclusion and the results published by the Trustees.

Policy

'To give away money is an easy matter, and in any man's power. But to decide to whom to give it, and how large and when, and for what purpose and how, is neither in every man's power – nor an easy matter.' This quotation from Aristotle was printed at the beginning of the Trust's Ninth Report.

The Trust's First Report was issued in 1957, covering the period from 1937 to 1956, during which it had disbursed just over £1 million on medical research, on museums and libraries, and on research concerned with the history of medicine. In 1979 over £9 million was allocated, bringing the total since 1937 to over

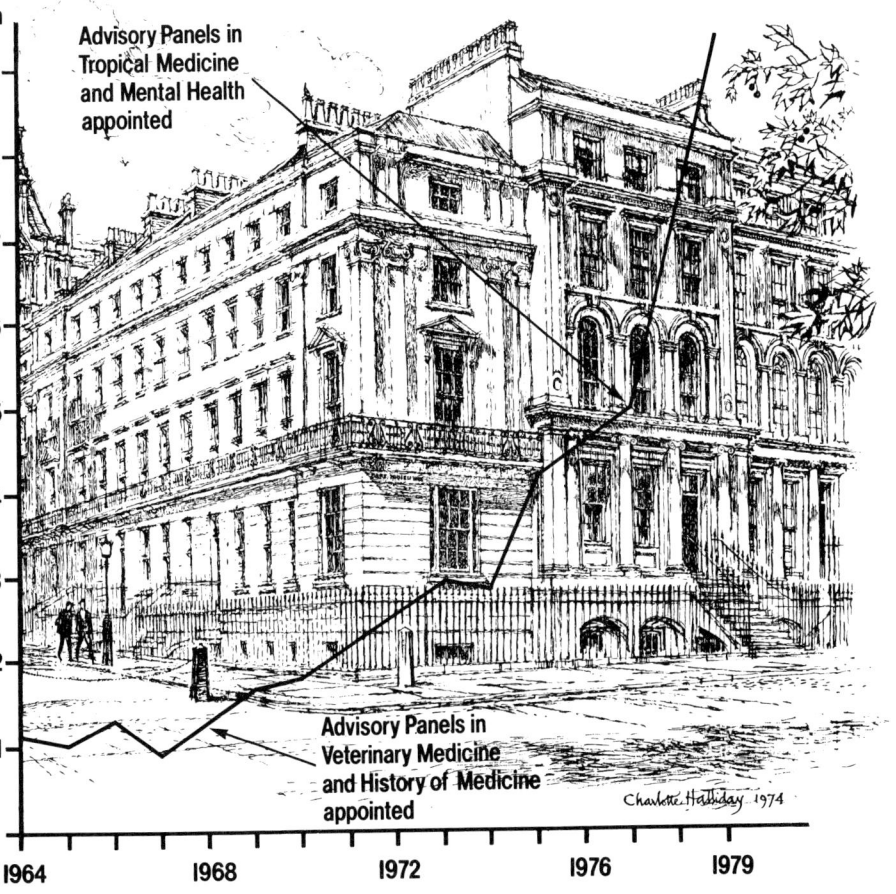

Advisory Panels in
Tropical Medicine
and Mental Health
appointed

Advisory Panels in
Veterinary Medicine
and History of Medicine
appointed

Charlotte Halliday 1974

1964   1968   1972   1976   1979

The Wellcome Trust allocation of funds 1964–1979, superimposed over the headquarters of the Wellcome Trust in London.

£50 million. Originally, priority was given to subjects in which Wellcome was especially interested: pharmacy, veterinary and tropical medicine, and the history of medicine, to which were later added experimental physiology, clinical biochemistry and biophysics. The Trust has always sought particularly to give support to important topics which were suffering from neglect. Veterinary research is one such area and this has been the subject of Wellcome scholarship and fellowship schemes and other programmes which have cost the

Trust nearly £3.5 million since 1968. Dermatology, another neglected discipline, received £750 000 between 1969 and 1976.

In 1964 the Robbins Report on the development of British universities was published. Among its recommendations was that the government should give more financial aid for the building of research accommodation and the purchase of modern scientific equipment. Prior to this a large proportion of the Wellcome Trust's funds had been allocated to buildings and equipment for scientific research but this type of support has now been reduced in favour of recurrent grants. Since 1937 over £5 million had been allocated in capital building grants and between 1946 and 1966, 105 new laboratories and extensions were erected using Wellcome money. Examples exist world-wide and include the Institute for Foot and Mouth Disease Research at Nairobi, Kenya; an extension to the Best Institute at the University of Toronto, Canada; an Institute of Medical Research at the University of Otago, New Zealand; a new wing for the Department of Biochemistry at the University of Cambridge; pharmacological laboratories at Yale University, USA; and laboratories at the School of Public Health at the University of Tehran, Iran.

Henry Wellcome's special interest in tropical medicine has been continued and expanded by the Trust, not only in the building of laboratories in Kenya, South India and Brazil, and in the equipment of laboratories and mobile units, but also in the establishment of units for research in several countries and the provision of a substantial number of grants for research on tropical diseases in the UK and overseas. Up to 1979, £5 640 000 has been allocated.

The central theme of the Trust's policy has remained the same through more than forty years. It is to support high quality research in human and animal medicine, maintaining a flexible approach so as to balance the support available from government and other bodies;

and above all to concentrate support where other sources are inadequate or where an innovative approach is needed. The role of this, the largest charitable foundation in Britain for the support of medical research, is of particular importance today when both medicine and higher education are largely a government monopoly.

In the future the Trust intends to continue this policy. The major part of its funds will be used to support medical research in the UK. Cut-backs in funding have produced severe problems for universities and the Trustees have recently introduced a scheme to fund high quality research workers at senior lecturer level, thereby releasing departmental funds and encouraging research. Support of medical research in tropical and under-developed countries remains an important part of the Trust's activities, and co-operation with European countries by the provision of travel grants and exchange fellowships will be encouraged. From time to time major awards are offered in areas which the Trustees have identified as needing special encouragement.

Types of Support for Medical Research

The support of research scientists by the Trust has taken a number of different forms over the years. In the Trust's early days the endowment of senior research posts helped to ensure that medical men at the top of their profession had the time and resources to do fundamental research work. There is a Wellcome Research Chair of Pharmacology at London University and a Wellcome Research Chair of Clinical Tropical Medicine at the London School of Hygiene and Tropical Medicine. Five-year research professorships have also been endowed at McGill University in Canada and at the University of Pennsylvania, USA. In 1961 the Trustees endowed a Research Professorship in Medical Science in memory of Sir Henry Dale at the Royal Society, of which he had been President. In recent years, this type of support has not been thought the most appropriate use of the Trust's funds.

In 1962 the Trust first awarded senior research fellowships in clinical science, and over the next fourteen years thirty-four were held by scientists who later achieved permanent senior appointments. Fellowships to provide surgeons and pathologists with research training are also provided. A large proportion of the Trust's funds is provided in response to applications received for research and technical assistance and expenses required for short-term projects in almost all branches of medical research.

The award of travel grants by the Trustees has helped to maintain collaboration and contact in medical research on a world-wide scale. Started in 1955, these grants now absorb £50 000 of Wellcome money each year, between 200 and 250 being awarded annually. They provide help with travel and subsistence costs for short visits to undertake research or learn new techniques and also travel expenses for workers going abroad on fellowships or short-term employment. The Trust has made contact with grant-giving bodies abroad so that a system of two-way communication can be arranged. Such schemes exist with New Zealand, Australia, South Africa, Canada and the United States. In the USA, the Burroughs Wellcome Fund, already referred to, provides the reciprocal arrangements. Research exchange in Europe has existed since 1957 when the Wellcome Trust began to work with the Danish Carlsberg Foundation, to which it is similar in origin and organization. Since then thirty-two exchange fellowships have been awarded by the two bodies. Similar arrangements with other European countries have resulted in 235 exchange fellowships from Europe and 74 to Europe being awarded.

The Trust has a special scheme whereby European and UK scientists engaged in related work can meet regularly and work in each other's laboratories. Since this programme was started in 1972 thirty awards have been made, and an agreement with the Mario Negri

Foundation in Milan enables Italian medical research workers to visit Britain for short periods.

Support for the History of Medicine

Over the years the Trust's policy towards the history of medicine has become increasingly directed towards academic research. The culmination of this policy was reached with the transfer of the Wellcome collection to the Science Museum in 1978. The Trust believed that it could not deal effectively with the great Wellcome collection and therefore decided to hand over the task to a national museum. Ten years earlier, in 1968, the Wellcome Historical Medical Museum and Library was renamed the Wellcome Institute for the History of Medicine in recognition of its research activities and services. Prior to this, in 1962, the Wellcome Library had been the subject of complete replanning and rehousing in the Wellcome Building in Euston Road and the American and Oriental rooms had been added. The Museum display was also greatly expanded.

In 1964 a sub-department for the history of medicine was established at University College, London, and this was followed in 1968 by the setting up of similar units at the Universities of Oxford and Cambridge. A lectureship in the history of medicine has also been recently established with Wellcome money at the University of Edinburgh. In 1976 an academic unit with four members was planned within the Wellcome Institute, to be integrated with the history of medicine unit at University College, London. The latest academic development in the Wellcome history of medicine programme has been the setting up in 1978 of a Contemporary Medical Archives Centre. Since the Second World War the Trust has made important grants towards the establishment of research museums and libraries of the history of medicine for other institutions. The Royal Colleges of Surgeons, of Obstetricians and Gynaecologists, and of Physicians, the Royal Society of Medicine, and other medical bodies, have been enabled to build, extend or re-equip museums and libraries with the Trust's assistance. Money has also been made available to support research and publication on a wide variety of medical historical topics, from medicine in the navy to Arabic and Roman medicine.

The Trustees and the Administration

There have been eighteen Trustees since 1937. Of these, Sir Henry Dale, OM, FRS, deserves special mention, for he was Chairman of the Trustees from 1938 until 1960, when he retired at the age of 85. Before this he had an outstanding scientific career, being awarded the Nobel Prize for Medicine in 1936. He was President of the Royal Society from 1940 to 1945. As Chairman of the Wellcome Trustees, he not only presided over the meetings of the Trustees but also undertook the day-to-day administration and correspondence until 1955, and remained closely concerned with all applications until his retirement. His immediate successor was Lord Piercy of Burford, a former director of the Bank of England who was also concerned with academic administration. In 1965 the Rt Hon. the Lord Franks, OM, GCMG, KCB, CBE, took over the Chairmanship. Lord Franks has been an academic and a diplomat, professor, university chancellor, head of an Oxford college, ambassador, and chairman of a bank. He has also served on both the Rockefeller Foundation and the Pilgrim Trust.

The administration of the Trust is in the hands of a director, who is also secretary to the Trustees, assisted by medical, scientific, and other professional and administrative staff. The staff have close links with other grant-giving bodies. For example, the current director was co-founder of the Association of Medical Research Charities in Great Britain, the Foundations Forum, and the Hague Club, an association of the chief executives of some of the major foundations in Europe.

Index

Index